SMOKE
&
MIROIRS

Steve Taylor

Smoke and Miroirs

Steve Taylor

Copyright © 2022

ISBN: 978-1-7396554-0-2

Published by Garfield House Publishing in conjunction with Writersworld. This book is produced entirely in the UK, is available to order from most book shops in the United Kingdom and is globally available via UK-based Internet book retailers and www.amazon.com.

This book is based on a true story, but names, certain characters and events have been added or changed.

Copy edited by Ian Large

Cover design by Jag Lall (www.jaglallart.com)

www.writersworld.co.uk

WRITERSWORLD

2 Bear Close Flats, Bear Close, Woodstock, Oxfordshire, OX20 1JX, United Kingdom
☎ 01993 812500
☎ +44 1993 812500

The text pages of this book are produced via an independent certification process that ensures the trees from which the paper is produced come from well managed sources that exclude the risk of using illegally logged timber while leaving options to use post-consumer recycled paper as well.

Thanks to:

Nick Bentley and Craig Holson

Prologue

I've never really understood why people want to be a Group Board Director.

Well, I kind of get it from an ego perspective and having the best bragging rights on the golf course, but apart from that, it seems like a lot of reading and responsibility for very little reward. They seem to just gather about six times a year, enjoy a fine culinary feast, then, the next day, stare at a screen with the Executive Summary on it for the duration of a meeting.

OK, maybe I do get it...

However, this band of merry ladies and gentlemen, for today at least, had the future of my business, and probably my career, in their hands. For today, I was proposing the national roll out of a pilot business in France that I had been creating and leading for the previous three years, that would cost many million euros of investment and take five years to complete. To say I was nervous was an understatement.

My name is Peter Simpson and I work for a company called Eastney Interiors Ltd., a business that sells kitchens to the trade.

On the day of the meeting in March 2019, I was up early – 4am early, much to the disgust of my long-suffering wife Kim, who didn't seem to understand why I wanted to be in London at 7am for a meeting that didn't start until 1pm. It was simple really; if I arrived at the office after 7.30am, there was very little chance of bagging one of the hot desks that were there for transient guests like me, and even less chance that the desk I could claim as mine would have any form of electrical or computer connectivity. The fact that I then had to sit there for six hours pretending to do some work was just a minor inconvenience.

The six hours dragged by extremely slowly, and I read my presentation for what must have been the four hundredth time. I wasn't even really reading it by that stage to be honest; I was just staring at words and numbers with my stomach turning like a tumble dryer.

I did drink an awful lot of tea that morning. It was something to do and gave me the opportunity to be in the office kitchen and pass the time of day with friends and colleagues that I rarely see. Unfortunately, too much tea means only one thing, and when the trips to the toilet started kicking in, I started panicking. I had a lengthy presentation to get through and to have to leave the room three times during it would probably appear less than professional to the audience.

The meeting started at 1pm, but I was then told that I wasn't on until about 3pm, so I had another two hours of pretending to be busy and chatting to people who, by now, were sick of the sight of me.

I was finally ushered in and took my seat. It might not have actually *been* three inches lower than everyone else's seat, but it felt like it to me. The chairman welcomed me and thanked me for the efforts that I had put into the business and the presentation I had prepared. He then said that the board had considered my proposal and were in favour of the investment. He followed that with a couple of operational questions and then started to move on to the next item on the agenda.

I said, 'Sorry, have we actually decided anything here?'

The rest of the room chuckled quietly, and the chairman said, 'Yes, go ahead and expand your business across France.'

I subsequently discovered that the lion's share of the debate among the board was actually done at the previous evening's feast, and that I had been fretting needlessly.

That was it. Ten minutes in and out. I was torn between being amazed at how little time it had taken and being utterly over the moon that a business that I had created in France, that should – by rights – never have worked in the first place, had been approved by the board for a national roll-out.

I shared a drink or two that night with a couple of people that had been with me from the beginning and had witnessed the moderate highs and crushing lows that go hand in hand with creating a business in France. As the evening passed and the wine flowed, a wonderful feeling started to sink in. After three years of struggle, chaos, fighting the market, the competition and often even my own team, I had done it. I had actually bloody well done it!

PART ONE
VIRGIN SNOW

1

The French business got off to a frosty start. Not in the weather sense, but in the atmosphere in my house.

I began with Eastney Interiors in the UK in 2002. A small group of us had created it from nothing and it had done rather well, so much so, that I had been asked to move to the USA by Bernard, the Group CEO, to set up Eastney Interiors in Florida. I went home that night and told Kim the news. She was pleased in the sense that it was a promotion for me, and she had always loved America, and what nicer part to move to than Florida? However, we had two grown-up daughters, one of whom had just had a child, and it meant leaving them all behind.

After a week or so of weighing up the pros and cons, we decided to give it a shot. It was probably a once in a lifetime opportunity, and Bernard was very generous in paying for trips backwards and forwards for the family.

So, in the autumn of 2013, we packed our bags and moved to the U.S of A. We had all our luggage and documentation and had put our house in Chichester on the market. It was a very tearful day, but we had already made plans for some of the family to come across in a month's time, so it didn't seem like the end of the world.

The first call that we received when we landed in Florida was from my father-in-law. He said that the minute our furniture was out of the house he had two offers of the full asking price. I was pleased, but I couldn't help wondering if our taste in furniture was really that bad! It wasn't going to be with us for six weeks, so we needed to go and buy some new stuff anyway, and I would be giving our furniture a long hard stare when it finally arrived.

With that news, we went straight to a duelling piano bar that we had made our social hub during our visits and sang our way through the jet lag. It was a tactic we were to frequently use with our guests when they landed in Orlando.

While I was busy setting up a kitchen business, Kim was busy setting up a home and a network of friends. She is much more open to general chit-chat than I am, so she was very good at getting us integrated into the local community and feeling part of the neighbourhood. We got involved in the street parties, of which there were many, and made some thoroughly good friends there.

I became very patriotic when I moved to Florida; I had Union Flag cups, T-shirts, clocks, posters and everything else you could imagine. My prized possession was a Union Flag camping chair that I would take out to each street party. It was particularly useful on each July Fourth when we would have our street Independence Day party. I would proudly sit in my brightly coloured chair declaring – very loudly – that I was, '...here to reclaim the land that is rightfully mine...' I was struck by more than one Oreo on those occasions.

We had really settled into our new life in Florida, so it was with a heavy heart that I had to call Kim while she was in the UK in October 2015 visiting the family, to tell her of a conversation I had just had with Bernard.

The American business had started well, and the board were anxious to see if there was a business to be had in Europe, starting with France, and as I had demonstrated that we could export the model once, they wanted me to leave the running of the American business to the locals and start again in Europe. Whilst I was proud that my achievements had been recognised, I had only lived in Florida for a couple of years, and now had to move back again.

I spent a good few hours going through the telephone call that I had to make in my head. I considered making myself out to be the victim in the hope that I would get some sympathy, and I considered making it a happy thing as if it was some sort of promotion.

I made myself a cup of tea and sat down with the phone. I was about to dial the number when I noticed that my shoes needed cleaning and decided that they should be done immediately. This was followed by other imperative tasks, such as emptying the bins, feeding the cat and ironing a shirt for the next day.

Having done all the jobs that I could reasonably do to avoid the inevitable, I sat down again with another cup of tea and made the call. I was going to talk my wife through every step of the discussion in a full, frank and honest way. I was going to be sympathetic, yet assertive and explain everything in detail, or at least that's what I thought. What actually fell out of my mouth when Kim picked up the phone was, 'Hey, guess what, we're moving to Kent.'

2

Bernard Jackson was a difficult man to please. For a start, he was most definitely a 'Bernard'; the British compulsion to reduce everyone's Christian name to one syllable just seeming inappropriate in this instance.

Born in Inverness, Bernard was a proud Scot. He didn't sound like one though; he had developed a perfect Queen's English accent over the years, and he had the stature and sonics that you instantly knew was of a man to be respected. People didn't mess with Bernard.

I think his business values came from his military background. Bernard did eight years in the Army in the '80s and '90s and had done two stints in Northern Ireland and one in the Gulf during that time. He rarely spoke about his time in the Army directly, and it isn't the sort of thing one asks about. He did, however, frequently speak about his acute frustrations caused by the centralised nature of the armed forces and how little the 'nobs', as he chose to call his glorious leaders, understood about the realities of daily life for the average squaddie. He resigned from the Army in 1993 and joined a national DIY company, quickly rising to the higher echelons with his ethos of empowering the people on the front line, and his hatred of central control and costs.

He had thoroughly earned the respect that people had for him. Not only did he have a meteoric rise within the DIY sector, but he had then led the creation of Eastney Interiors in the UK when Bullings Design, a national home improvement chain, wanted to open a dedicated trade subsidiary and decided that Bernard was the right person for the job.

With the help of a few disparate individuals like myself, he gathered a motley crew of about 50 people to start the business. As the business grew, there were the various in-house disasters that beset any company, and the small matter of a global recession. Despite that, the business that Bernard created didn't just survive, it thrived. So much so, that he was appointed CEO of Bullings in 2007. He gained a respect within the square mile for being someone that always delivered on his promises, and it was a privilege for me to have been a part of that story. I – like many others – always went the extra mile for Bernard.

3

Eastney Interiors evolved considerably under Bernard's leadership. Bullings' product range was largely concentrated on items such as blinds, drapes, curtains, flooring and some basic furniture, like drawers and tables. They had recently also started selling some basic flatpack kitchen units, with limited success.

Bernard had identified that the products that a builder was likely to purchase from the Bullings range were the ones where the homeowner lacked the desire or ability to install it themselves, such that there was an opportunity for the builder to add value and make money. This meant that items like curtains and drapes were of no use, but on the other hand, the flooring, kitchen units and blinds were most definitely areas to focus on, and maybe expand.

With a largely increased flooring and kitchen range, Bernard carved a trade business out. As the range evolved though, it was diverging significantly from the Bullings range and some of the economies of scale were being lost. The landscape was clouded, however, by the fact that the sales at Eastney Interiors were growing exponentially, and the product ranges stocked were delivering far higher margins than those at Bullings, with kitchens proving to be the golden egg. This led to considerable conflict within the boardroom at Bullings, which along with the success of Eastney Interiors, culminated in the appointment of Bernard as CEO of the parent company in 2007.

4

To get things moving in France, I appointed a second-in-command from the UK business, a guy called Sean Bond. He was a Yorkshireman but had lived and worked in France for five years in the late 1980s. He had long since grown tired of the James Bond jibes but had developed a more than passable impression of Sean Connery over the years, and a near encyclopaedic knowledge of the film franchise.

Sean had a degree in French from Leeds University, which was clearly going to help in the development of a business in France. When I asked him how he ended up selling kitchens to builders having spent several years in languages, he said that he found learning languages easy. He also spoke German and Spanish to A-level standard. While he was in France, he did a bit of teaching and also worked in a DIY store. He said he preferred the DIY store, so when he came back to the UK he got a job with a home improvement company that had international subsidiaries where he may be able to add value and carve out a long-term future.

Along the way, he discovered that a friend of his, who had joined Eastney Interiors, was earning about 20 per cent more than him and, being a true Yorkshireman, Sean decided to abandon the long-term plan and follow the money.

5

It was March 2016, and after a couple of meetings in the UK, Sean and I each packed a bag and went over to France for a first look, to try to get a sense of the challenge ahead.

It was a wet Wednesday lunchtime, and we were sat in a café in Paris after having had a quick drive around the industrial areas to see who our competitors were. To be honest, it wasn't overly obvious. We could see companies that served the trade, and we could see companies that sold kitchens, but we couldn't see many companies that sold *kitchens* to the *trade*. There was clearly more work to be done on this matter.

Over coffee and a sandwich, we started to plan. Our UK legal team had spoken to one of their advisors who also had offices in Paris and, through them, we had lined up a meeting with a Madame Dupont at 3pm at the Rue du Colisée in the 8th Arrondissement. As a lawyer she had assisted in setting up UK companies in France before and knew a few people that could probably help us. We looked up her address on a map and it didn't look too far away from where we currently were.

One of the many things that annoys my wife about me is that I am always way too early for everything. I've never seen the point in planning to arrive just in time, only to have your plans thwarted by traffic or other such uncontrollable events. This means that I spend rather too much time hanging around at my destinations. Today was different though.

My company car at that time was an E-class Mercedes. I was very proud to have it and tried to take good care of it. It was only six months old and in very good condition. This made me slightly nervous driving around Paris as the streets are either three kilometres wide, like the Champs-Élysées, or three metres wide with cars parked... sorry, dumped everywhere. The area around the lawyer's office was in the latter category, and while there is plentiful underground parking around Paris generally, the entrances are all incredibly narrow and the turning circles required are that of the roundabout at the Savoy Hotel in London. Consequently, I spent about half an hour trying to find a parking space on the roadside, which ate into the extra time I had allowed. We finally arrived ten minutes late.

The offices in Rue du Colisée were on the 5th floor with no lift. Once inside, I was struck by how dark and old the offices looked. The walls were all panelled in what looked like teak from floor to ceiling, and the lighting was provided by a single ornate chandelier that looked like it had been there since Paris was built. I approached the receptionist, who was behind an enormous desk, made of the same material as the panels, and announced our arrival. I started to apologise for our tardiness, but she just beckoned us to some chairs with the back of her hand and said, 'Wait there.'

A further 15 minutes later, Madame Dupont emerged and called us through to her office, which looked identical to the one we had just been in. We all sat down and shared some small talk over a coffee, during which I told the story of our parking, and the subsequent late arrival on our part. She just shrugged her shoulders and said that, in her experience, if a meeting in France is due to start at 2pm, what the average French person understands by that is 'some time before 3pm'. Fair enough – Lesson Number One.

Madame Dupont was very helpful. She was going to be able to connect us with a recruitment agent who would in turn be able to get us some expertise in areas like HR, finance, property sourcing and product purchasing. This would be enough to get us going for now. As her area of expertise was the legal side of things, she was able to create the business for us and make sure that we had the correct permissions and documentation in place. I was to be the *Président-Directeur Général* of the new enterprise, and the other board director was to be the UK Finance Director, Fiona Harris. We needed to get a bank account going, but Fiona could do that through our UK banking partners, and we had to get some capital sent across to get started.

Throughout our discussions with Madame Dupont, I was conscious of the fact that there was never any invitation to call her by her first name. I knew it was Isabelle, because it was on her business card, but when I called her Madame Dupont, at no time did she encourage me to be more informal. I assumed that she felt she needed to maintain the impression of formality and professionalism indicated by the décor and surroundings. During our meeting, Sean and I would occasionally say something light-hearted and laugh, whereas Madame Dupont would make the smallest indication of a smile that she could possibly get away with, before moving the conversation along. However, in terms of productivity, it had been a good meeting – so far.

The next topic of conversation was an understanding of our trading model, which meant that I had to spend a half hour or so explaining how we go about things in Eastney Interiors Ltd. She was aware of the broad idea that we sold kitchens to builders from industrial estates but knew nothing of the nitty gritty.

In short, the business model is one of local empowerment and strong relationships between the depot team and the local builders. Each depot manager recruits their own team, sets prices on a deal-by-deal basis, and is paid a percentage of the depot profits each month. The model had been very well received in the UK and had been one of the strongest selling points for recruitment in Florida.

Madame Dupont made plentiful notes during my informal presentation and asked many questions along the way, which led to more notes. When I had finally finished, she looked at her notes, then at me, then sighed, before she said some words which hit me like a thunderbolt: 'On the basis of what you have just said Mr Simpson, your business model is illegal in France.'

6

That night, Sean and I were staying at the Imperial Etoile, near the Arc de Triomphe in Paris. We had researched many hotels before we travelled that morning and had decided to call this one 'home'. It had underground parking which turned out to be easy to use, at least by Paris car park standards anyway, and was very close to the Périphérique. It was also a short walk away from an Irish bar and an Indian restaurant, and that ticked a lot of our boxes. It wasn't what you would call a 'relationship hotel'; I don't think I ever saw the same person more than once apart from behind the hotel bar, but it was good enough for us.

We were in the Irish bar next door to the hotel – McGuires – and were still digesting the news from Madame Dupont that our business model was illegal. She had pointed out that we were unable to have deal-by-deal pricing as everything had to be transparent. This was due to the fact that we could be investigated by the authorities if a customer felt that we were being preferential to other customers, thus creating an unfair advantage. The French market demanded that you have a price list which is visible to all, and discounts from that are only allocated based on individual customer spend.

We also discovered that we could not sell any product below the price that we had paid for them. Whilst you may wonder why you would want to do that in the first place, there are times when you take a decision to do a super-low price on something as a loss leader to try to get to a conversation about their kitchen business. A sprat to catch a mackerel as it were. Not in France though. Again, the authorities could land at any time to inspect our paperwork and, as the head of the business, I could easily end up in court.

There were also some things which, whilst not illegal, were going to add significant costs to the business compared to the UK. These were primarily around labour costs and labour laws generally.

The French are renowned for their 35-hour week, although it was only enshrined in law in the year 2000. The reason for introducing it was to create more employment by job sharing, but it didn't work out like that. A member of staff can work more than 35 hours, but after that it is considered overtime and can be very costly to the employer.

So-called 'white collar workers' are not restricted by the 35-hour week, but they are only allowed to work 218 days a year. The principle being that employees all work about the same amount of time, but that management need to be more flexible. A complete two-week cycle of who is working which shift, whilst complying with the employment hours laws, needs to be on the office notice board in all business areas, in case – once again – the authorities visit you to inspect it.

Sean and I couldn't help but find this funny. It was a defence mechanism we were going to rely on a lot in the months and years ahead. We had visions of teams of special government agents descending from helicopters, all guns blazing, demanding that we all lay face down on the floor while a little man with glasses checked a sales estimate we had provided the previous Tuesday, whilst in the next depot, a similar group of armed men in balaclavas with calculators were diligently checking that the total hours on the rota didn't exceed 35 for any one person.

7

It was clear that we needed to do some fine tuning, to say the least, if we were going to be able to trade in France, and seeing as the biggest hurdles seemed to be around people and pricing, it was priority number one to get a human resources expert and a product expert to speak to.

The recruitment agent that Madame Dupont had introduced us to was a man named Didier Couque, and we were able to meet up with Didier the next morning in the Imperial. Didier was a cheerful and engaging individual, and with a Cheshire Cat grin that, I suspected, he had perfected over the years to help calm the nerves of the people he was interviewing. The conversation with Didier was relaxed and enjoyable. He was currently self-employed, working as a consultant to companies needing short-term help, but was always on the lookout for a position to come along that he could invest time and energy in to create something worthwhile. During our conversation, I said that I needed a product expert as soon as possible, to which Didier said, 'How about an hour's time?' When asked how he could magic a product expert out of thin air so quickly, he said that he knew a guy called Henri that had relevant experience and was currently available. Didier said that at the very least Henri would be able to point us in the right direction.

I've always believed in doing something today that you can improve tomorrow, rather than trying to get everything nailed down before you take a step forward. It was something that Bernard had instilled in me many years ago and was essential when you were driving through virgin snow, which was exactly what we were doing right now. So, on that basis, and because we had no other options at that stage, I suggested a lunch for Didier, Henri, Sean and myself to agree on the way forward. Didier said that he knew a very good place about a kilometre away, where he knew the owner and we would be looked after. He said he would drive, and he called Henri to arrange to meet up at the restaurant.

Didier's driving was not for the faint-hearted. I was in the front passenger seat, a decision I immediately regretted. What I would have given right then to be unable to see what was going on in front of us. I felt a great degree of sympathy for the other poor road users around us, be they in a car, on a cycle or even just attempting the reckless act of crossing the street. I counted four occasions in about five minutes where, if the other party hadn't taken evasive action, there would have been a collision. Didier's response to each of them was to sound his horn and raise his outstretched hand to the windscreen, palm inwards like he was counting to five, as if asking, 'What are you doing, idiot?' It was the first time I had seen that particular gesture, but it does seem to be the default reaction of all French drivers when confronted with something they aren't expecting.

Along the route, we approached a set of red lights and he drove straight through them without slowing or looking. I turned round to see if Sean had noticed this attempt on our lives, but he had his head in his hands as if someone had just shouted, '*Brace, brace!*'

I said to Didier, 'Did you not see that red light?' to which he replied, 'Aah, that's the difference between you and me. You are English and saw the red light as an instruction, whereas I am French and saw it as a request.'

8

French restaurant food falls into two broad categories. There's the general bistro fare such as steak and chips, croque monsieur/madame, andouillette sausage, quiche Lorraine and the like. These will almost always be served with a side salad and bread. The menu in these establishments seldom varies and the food and service are such that the customer can travel to the restaurant, order and eat their lunch, and get back to their home or workplace within their defined lunch break. This type of fare is often well received by my British colleagues, such that it is frequently remarked that 'We could learn a lot from the French about lunch.'

In reality, if you look at the clientele in these places, you will see they are usually older people, for whom a more formal sit-down eating experience is a tradition they grew up with and is more about the break from the daily toils, and having some decent conversation, than it is about the food.

Unfortunately for the traditionalist, bistros are closing down at an alarming rate. This is in large part because the younger generation – whilst not opposed to bistro fare – are now much more likely to choose on-the-go fast food for lunch over traditional French food. I've noticed though, that the younger people lament the decline of the bistro in much the same way that the British lament the loss of the corner shops, blissfully ignoring the fact that they only closed down because we all decided to drive past 18 of them every week on our way to Tesco.

The other category of French food is the gastronomic dining experience. I think you need to separate the food from the experience to understand it properly. The menu is often unfathomable, in that it gives you the merest clue as to what will be served. Whatever you order is likely to be small and in the middle of an unnecessarily large plate surrounded by a very artistic swirl of 'jus' and some foam or other. There will likely be a small potato and another, unidentifiable, vegetable peeking out from under the main item you ordered. The food will be edible.

To unpick the experience though, is to start to understand the French as a nation.

The chef will see himself as much an artist as a cook. He will have studied his art either formally or will have learnt his trade from previous generations of artists. His reputation in the local community and in the wider community of chefs is much more important to him than the quality of the meal he serves you. If a customer doesn't enjoy their meal, it will be because the customer lacks the palette and sophistication required. It will never be because the meal was poor.

The menu is deliberately vague, this is a part of the game. A French person will never ask the waiter for any explanation or clarity, as this would expose themselves as a member of the *hoi polloi*, and that would never do. As a Brit though, I was allowed this concession – in fact, they expect nothing less from us. Secretly though, my French friends would all be listening to the answers I received so that they could amend their own order accordingly.

Having ordered the food, next comes the wine. It is more than acceptable to ask questions about the wine, it is also a part of the game. The waiter or sommelier will respect a customer for asking the 'right' questions about which wine to order. Questions like whether the *Château Canon 2007* will be better with the beef than the *Château Pape Clément 2017,* will allow the waiter to display his knowledge of the subject matter to his audience. The person ordering the wine then needs to pause for a few seconds, to properly digest the expert advice provided, before selecting their wine. The waiter will then nod, retrieve the carte du vin, say, 'Excellent choice Sir,' and disappear.

When the wine appears, there is more theatre to be observed. The wine will be shown to the host and uncorked. The waiter will smell the cork and put it on a small plate by the host's side. Then, he will pour a small amount to be sampled, and it must be the host that samples the wine. This is not the work of a moment either. First, the taster should check the 'legs' of the wine by swirling it in the glass. Then, when it has settled, he will take a hearty sniff. The taster must nod in approvement at all times during this show. Finally, the wine should be tasted, with the host nodding profusely, before eventually saying 'perfect'. The other guests at the table must watch this show in silence, as if they were watching a surgeon remove a kidney. Only when the host has approved the wine may conversation resume, as the host no longer requires the keen concentration required for this most important regime. Then, and only then, will everyone get their – usually very small – glass of wine.

The food will eventually appear. No comment must be made about how long the food is taking, in much the same way that no-one ever said to Michelangelo, '...come on Mickey-boy, get a wriggle on!' Upon arrival, the food must be looked at from all angles and comment must be made about the beauty of the presentation.

After the meal has been finished, all guests must wax lyrical about the multi-sensory experience this has been, before the host settles the bill with a second mortgage, and no more than a cursory glance at the total. The bill must not, under any circumstances, be studied.

The fine dining experience is one way that the French have of showing their social status. Within the confines of an overtly socialist framework, one must be careful about how one displays one's superiority and wealth, and the gastronomic restaurant is an excellent and acceptable arena in which to perform.

9

The restaurant we were in was a bistro that Didier and Henri used when they worked together and where they still caught up with ex-colleagues now and again. We were introduced to the owner, Monsieur Laurent, who seemed very happy to meet us and we sat in what, I assumed, was their normal table, as we walked in a particular direction without any guidance or conversation.

It was quite a small bistro and there were probably two or three more tables than there should have been for everyone's comfort. A bottle of red wine arrived almost immediately without being asked for and, after a brief taste by Didier, a glass was poured for all.

It is very rare for me to take wine with lunch, but today, and more specifically, after the near-death experience of our journey here, I took a hearty slug. Sean said he'd like a beer as well, so I joined him. We deserved it.

The French don't seem to view the taking of beer or wine with lunch as 'drinking'. They think nothing of having a few glasses of wine or beer, before driving back to the office and starting work again. The French have stricter drink drive laws than in the UK, but as they don't see it as drinking, I guess they don't consider that the drink drive limits apply in that situation. I used to imagine the situation if someone was stopped by the local gendarme on the way back to the office:

'Excuse me sir, have you been drinking?'
'No officer.'
'But you were driving rather erratically. Would you mind blowing into this please?'
'Of course, officer.'
'Oh, sir, according to this you are in excess of the legal limit of alcohol to drive.'
'That's impossible, I only had two glasses of wine and a beer with lunch.'

'"Lunch" you say?'
'Yes, lunch.'
'Aaah, you should have said sir, sorry to have bothered you.'

10

We needed to get moving with the business, and quick. It was now March and we wanted to be open at the beginning of October. Even though the retail kitchen market has historically focussed on the January sales, the trade kitchen market has different drivers.

Eastney Interiors was created completely around the things that matter to the trade customer. Things like credit terms and locally available stock are business critical to him to be able to 'get in, get out and get paid'. The locally held stock is probably the single biggest thing he requires. Most people don't mind waiting six weeks or so for their shiny new kitchen to be delivered. After all, it's a majorly disruptive project and requires considerable planning. When something goes wrong, doesn't fit, or is damaged though, householders' patience with suppliers wears thin pretty quick – they need a replacement today, and by today, they mean that literally. Eastney's ability to provide that to the builder means that he can finish the job on time, get paid, and be seen as a saviour by the householder. This results in recommendations for the builder within local networks and neighbourhoods, and therefore more sales for Eastney Interiors. Many home owners don't even know where their kitchen came from, they just know that it was supplied by the wonderful builder that did Mrs Smith's kitchen across the road.

The way Eastney priced kitchens was also completely aligned to the requirements of the small builder. With a high list price which is visible to all, and deep discounts from that, which are confidential to each builder, there is an opportunity for the builder to apply a handling charge, or commission to the price that he paid us for the products. Whether or not they choose to avail themselves of that opportunity is up to them, but it is there none the less.

Regarding workload, again Eastney Interiors had set its stall out to support the small local builder. In communities where Christmas is a celebrated festival, the day itself is a major focus point. Families get together and many social gatherings take place. With the kitchen increasingly being the heart of the home and where people gather and socialise, having a kitchen to be proud of is extremely important. This creates an 'end date' for our trade customer to work to.

Builders don't just fit kitchens of course; at any given time, they are looking for work, pricing up for work, preparing for the next job, doing the job they are on, finishing off the last job, and collecting the money for the job they did before that. They are extremely busy people and any help they can get from suppliers in reducing their stress is very gratefully received. That is before you bring into the equation the three overriding factors that can land at any time and destroy their plans: the weather, emergencies, and over running jobs.

For all that, there is still a natural flow to a builder's year. Home owners tend to want outdoor work done in the summer for obvious reasons, and when a builder is working on his own development, it makes sense to use the long days and better weather to build the home or extension they are working on and make it waterproof before winter. This tends to create a natural window for kitchens to be fitted in people's homes between the end of summer and Christmas. Hence our target of opening in early October.

11

At this stage, I hadn't yet agreed any terms or commitment to Didier and Henri. I wanted to get a sense of how they were going to deal with our issues and of their personal work ethic. To do that, Sean and I needed to take a while to explain what life in Eastney Interiors was like, both in the depots and in the support functions. I was going to lead the recruitment for the support team, and Sean was going to take the lead with the depot staff. We were going to open ten depots in October. I knew that it was going to be ten depots because Bernard used to call me every other day to remind me.

The support staff required were across the board. We would outsource where we could for things like payroll and IT specialists, but we still needed to find about ten people. Didier explained his process for recruiting in France; he used a combination of online awareness and traditional 'poaching'. I was getting a good feeling about Didier, he seemed like a guy that got the job done. Well, at the very least, he talked a good fight.

When Sean had finished explaining the type of people we were looking for as depot managers, he touched upon the point that, in the UK, there were trade kitchen suppliers which we could use to try to recruit staff from and that, as yet, we hadn't found those companies in France. Sean and I were going out again the next day to drive around some more industrial estates.

Henri barely looked up from his entrecôte steak and said in a very matter-of-fact way, 'I wouldn't bother if I were you; builders in France don't buy kitchens.'

12

Back in McGuires that night, Sean and I were staring dejectedly into our pints. In the space of a week, we had discovered that our business model was illegal and that our customer didn't exist. Apart from that, everything looked good. Well, when I say that, the Indian restaurant had turned out to be a real find, and that must count as a positive... mustn't it?

Sean was slightly more positive than me, in that having lived and worked in France before, his experience told him that everything seemed to be a problem at first in France, and then, somehow, miraculously, a way through could usually be found. Whilst I got that as a general concept, the two issues we were facing at that moment did seem to be deal-breakers to me. I decided to call Bernard. The hour's difference in time meant that it was still a civilised time to call the UK.

There are two sides to Bernard. On some occasions, he is tough as nails, leaving people in meetings quite aware of his displeasure. He has a natural presence about him that makes people nervous, and he is not intimidated by rank or supposed expertise. He can also smell complacency at a hundred metres and deal with it swiftly and effectively.

On a different day though, he could be the most considerate, charming, charismatic, witty and supportive leader you could wish for. He invests heavily in people and is not overly perturbed by mistakes. He frequently used the expression, 'We often fail our way forwards.' He was the sort of person you want to look up to in times of crisis; indeed, he was Churchillian in many ways.

The trouble was, you never quite knew which Bernard you were going to get on any given day.

When I had explained the situation to Bernard, he was quite clear. He said, 'Peter, as I see it, you can either spend a small fortune on market research, or you can spend the same money on testing it for yourself. Which do you want to do?' I said that I wanted to test it myself and he said, 'OK, me too, let's do it.'

Back in the bar, Sean had refreshed our glasses and I told him what Bernard had said. It gave us both a huge leap in confidence. We were going to *fight them on the beaches*.

The next day, Friday, I had another meeting with Didier in the Imperial. I agreed terms with him, and he was able to start in two weeks' time. Whilst I didn't yet have a strong view either way on Henri, Didier spoke very highly of him, and as Didier was my 'people person', I needed to learn to trust his judgement. Henri could start immediately. We then discussed the other positions we needed to fill and the salary packages available. We had to act quickly, so we decided that we would go for the people we could get fairly quickly, as opposed to the potentially perfect candidate that might be on a six- or twelve-month notice period. Again, do something today that you can improve tomorrow. I said that the most critical of these recruits was the finance director, and that the broader background that person had, the better. We could push the budget a bit on this person as I expected to sweat that particular asset quite hard. Given the criteria I had given Didier, I was nervous that I was asking too much. When I raised this point with him, Didier just said, 'Leave it to me, there's always a way in France.' I knew at that point that Didier and I were going to get along just fine.

Then, I called Madame Dupont and gave her the instruction to commence with the legals. She said that she would but before she did, she wanted to write to me to confirm the advice she had given me before, regarding the business model legality, or lack of it. I called Fiona and asked her to set up the bank account and transfer the capital. We were off to the races.

13

With the green light having been given to the business, it was time to get to know our new product and marketing manager a little better, so I asked him to meet me in the Imperial on the Monday after I had spoken to Madame Dupont.

Henri Daix was not an easy man to read. He certainly wasn't as effusive as Didier. He seemed to be a more thoughtful individual who kept his cards close to his chest. I asked him to give me a summary of his experience as I've never been keen on reading CVs.

He had been in product and marketing for his whole career, most recently as director for both departments within a national kitchen retailer. Prior to that, he had worked in various businesses such as a clothing retailer, a restaurant chain and a flooring company, and it was in the flooring company that he had worked with Didier.

I was interested to hear about the kitchen company in more detail and I wanted to know why he had left, but I didn't want to ask directly. This didn't matter, as he was very happy to talk about his experiences and the team he had built up around him. He was very proud of the people he worked with and the achievements they had accomplished together.

He was still cautious about what he was saying though. He would speak passionately about a particular achievement and get slightly animated, and then he would suddenly stop, as if he believed he had said too much.

I've learned to be comfortable with awkward silences. Frequently, saying nothing is the loudest and most effective statement you can make. There are many people that feel the need to fill quiet space with words, but I am not one of them. When Henri went quiet during his talk, I just let it hang until he started speaking again.

When he got to the part of the story regarding his departure, it seemed to me that he was uncomfortable talking about it. It transpired that he wasn't uncomfortable talking about it; he was actually still very emotional about it and wanted to make sure he still spoke rationally.

The French kitchen company he worked for was purchased by a Chinese company who grew by acquisition. The French business was the fourth European one that they had bought in the previous three years. Within three months of the takeover, the Chinese had replaced the president of the French business with a Chinese national, and many of the operational functions within the business were centralised back in Beijing. Product and marketing were two of those functions and so Henri was made redundant.

The new management of the business decided that a way to increase profitability was to have as little local support and management as possible and, to that end, there were numerous additional redundancies, many of whom were in Henri's old team.

By the way Henri told his story, it was clear that he still felt very bitter, not necessarily about his own demise, although he definitely wasn't happy about it, but more that the team he had built up had been systematically dismantled and that good people had lost their livelihoods.

What I saw here was a man that had unfinished business, and would work night and day to create a serious competitor to the Chinese. Perfect.

14

After an hour or so of getting to know Henri, I could see that Didier was right about him. He was a committed and thorough individual, deeply knowledgeable about our sector and determined to make our business successful.

I was very keen to hear why French builders were so different to British and American builders in that they didn't buy any kitchens, so I asked Henri to give me the story.

He told me that when 'Baron' Haussmann was rebuilding Paris in the 1850s and '60s, it was at the same time as the re-emergence of the French Bourgeoisie post-revolution. In the new classless society that underpinned French life, people were creating class in different ways. One of these ways was in cooking, or should I say, not cooking.

People in those times who could afford to, ate out a lot. It was a way to demonstrate your class and wealth while mixing with like-minded people. This meant that no space was required in the newly-created homes that Haussmann was building for a kitchen. The rationale was that you didn't need anywhere in your home dedicated to preparing food, any more than you needed space in your home for repairing a bicycle. The minimum legal requirement at that time (and still today) was a *'point d'eau'*, basically just a sink and tap, and it would be tucked away in a very small space indeed.

The Haussmann-style buildings took over Paris and then spread to other large conurbations. You can easily spot them today as they are all no higher than six storeys and have balcony rails on the second and fifth floors.

Over the decades following the Haussmann era, people slowly decided they wanted some kitchen space, so newer buildings were constructed with a dedicated kitchen area, and in the homes that Haussmann built, people were re-purposing a room, usually sacrificing a bedroom. Still though, the minimum requirement for any new home was the *point d'eau*, so that is what all new homes were equipped with. The consequence of this was that when someone bought a new home, one of the first things they did was to install a kitchen or buy a selection of free-standing cupboards. For this, they had to visit their local *cuisiniste* or furniture shop. This meant that all kitchen sales, regardless of whether they were initiated by a new construction, or a private refurbishment, ended up in the retail sector, and builders never needed to buy a kitchen. It sounded to me like kitchens were viewed more as items of furniture than a fixture of the house, and why would you need a builder to help you buy furniture?

Henri quoted me a statistic that 97% of all kitchen sales in France went through the retail channels, with 3% being defined as trade. 'Oh,' I said, laughing, 'so it's not *all* bad news then!'

15

I was starting to get to know Sean as we spent time together driving around France. Recently divorced and with no children, the idea of starting again in a different location quite appealed to him. He was combining his time looking around builders' merchants for staff, with driving around different parts of Paris to decide where he wanted to live. I had agreed with Bernard that we would pay to rent a flat for him with regular trips back to the UK all the time that the business was in pilot mode. As soon as we went to develop it, Sean would have to move to France permanently or transfer back to the UK. This meant that he didn't have to sell his home in York all the time that we were developing the business. I didn't see why Sean had to go through the domestic upheaval that I had, just for the sake of a few years. He was fine with this, indeed grateful for the opportunity in France along with the domestic arrangements.

While we were in other merchants' outlets, I would usually walk around looking at product range and at how French customers interacted with the staff in these businesses. At the same time, Sean would be pretending to be an English builder setting up a business in France and asking the staff about the range of products and services that the companies offered. This gave him the opportunity to flush out any that spoke English, as Sean would dumb down his French for this exercise. Whilst it wasn't essential for the depot managers to speak English, I was mindful of the fact that Bernard would very much like to be able to converse directly with the first few managers, and it would make *my* life immeasurably easier if Bernard could talk directly to them as well!

Sean was going to be the first area manager for the business. This was for two reasons. Firstly, I would be making Sean responsible for delivering the sales on a daily basis, so it was imperative that he had full control over which people we recruited for Day One. Secondly, it gave us time to see how each depot manager performed, not just in terms of sales, but in terms of character and adaptability before we decided who would be the first French area manager.

The first few people that Sean identified as possible recruits all happened to not be straightforward dyed-in-the-wool French people. Each of them had a slightly different story, either being first- or second-generation immigrants or by having mixed parentage. While this wasn't in itself a problem, it did raise some interesting questions. Eastney Interiors was a business based on relationships, and if we were trying to appeal to French artisans that had studied their trade for many years before gaining their qualifications, were we not better looking for people with a similar background? Also, would the business be scalable if it depended on such backgrounds and attitudes?

I decided that traction was more important than scalability at that stage of development and agreed with Sean that we would take on the six people that he had identified. They could all start on various dates in May, but all chose to start on the first of June. I thought this odd, until Didier told me of the mechanics of the French working year, and May in particular.

French bank holidays are almost all on fixed dates and there are three of them in May. In the UK, most bank holidays are on Mondays, but in France they are strict about them being on the correct date, resulting in them popping up on any day of the week. This fact means that they actually lose their day off if it falls on a weekend. The other side of that coin is that bank holidays are more disruptive to business when they land mid-week. Alongside this is the fact that the French holiday year ends at the end of May each year. Just to add more issues, the people we were looking at were all on the 218-day contract and had amassed many lieu days over the year with their former employer, which all had to be used up by the end of May as well. I was also informed of the French tradition of 'faire le pont' or to make a bridge between a weekend and a bank holiday by using accrued lieu days.

The consequence of these planets aligning, is that May is very much a holiday month, and the reason that our new recruits didn't want to start until June was that they didn't want to miss out on any time off. I was starting to get a sense of French priorities.

16

It was now the end of April, and I was in the Imperial Hotel looking at the piles of kitchen suppliers' literature, trying to make sense of them, when Didier called to tell me that he had identified a potential finance director, a chap called Claude Houllier. He was currently finance manager at a nationwide chain of convenience stores but had become frustrated with the lack of potential for personal development. Didier had briefly explained our set up, so Claude had looked up the UK company online and decided that this could be the position for him. Helpfully for me, he also had experience of audit, having been group auditor for a hotel chain along the way. Audit covers a multitude of disciplines, not least being corporate governance, and this experience would be very useful to me.

There were a couple of problems. Claude was a very keen golfer, and he was due to fly to the USA the next day with his family to take a road tour for a few weeks, culminating in watching the PGA championship in Oklahoma. The other problem was that he was on a three-month contract with his current employer.

Either way, I had to get to his home town of Lille from where I was in Paris pretty quickly if I wanted to meet him before he left. He finished work at 5pm and had agreed to meet me in the Crest International Hotel in Lille at 6pm for a coffee and a chat, so I immediately took the TGV from Paris to Lille, a fantastic service made even better by the fact that the station in Lille is directly across the road from the Crest.

At some points in life we have to be a salesperson. Whether that is selling in the pure sense in a work environment, or selling an idea to an investor, or just selling yourself to a potential employer or even a domestic partner. There's no avoiding it, and the job for Sean and myself in the early days, and certainly before there was even a business to show people, was to 'sell the dream'. This wasn't helped by just about everybody that we spoke to at that stage saying exactly the same thing: '...but builders don't buy kitchens in France.'

Claude was no different, but I explained that there was one supplier that sold kitchens to builders that we had identified; they were called Cuisinex, who were primarily a retailer, but also sold to the trade if required. While we couldn't find any builders that had ever actually used them, or ever seen any builders driving around with kitchens on their vans, the fact that they existed at all was enough to placate most people at this stage, thankfully.

Claude could talk. Heavens above, he could talk. After about an hour of him telling me about his background, almost without pausing for breath, I felt that there couldn't possibly be anything more to know. What his unending monologue did though, was to tell me about what was important to him in his work life. He needed a sense that he wasn't just ticking boxes but was actually shaping his environment. He needed to go home at night believing that we were further forward this evening than we were this morning. He wanted to have a team around him that he could lead and hopefully inspire.

I liked what I heard, and he asked all the right questions of me in terms of how we were going to get a group of people around us that had a common goal.

When it came to discussing packages, he was unusually candid with me about his salary and bonus arrangements. Whilst I couldn't offer long-term incentives at this stage, I could certainly offer an initial salary, bonus and car package that was in excess of his current deal. We shook hands that night. I was going to get Didier to email him an offer letter tomorrow, and he was going to resign while he was on holiday.

I now had an HR director, a product director, an operations director, a finance director and six managers, all inside about a month. It was time to address the elephant in the room in that our business model was illegal in France and I would end up in court if we didn't change it.

17

I was discovering that Sean and I viewed things from very different angles, and I liked that. I tend to take a broad-brush approach and just think about the direction of travel to the detriment of the detail, whereas Sean tends to think of the consequential implications of every action, sometimes to the detriment of our objectives. We both benefitted from having the other in the room. I think my standpoint originated in my fundamental lack of patience, and Sean's originated from spending far too many hours and evenings reading about conspiracy theories on the internet. We spent many an hour sat in Paris traffic discussing the Moon landing, JFK, Lady Diana and such like. He would always preface his outlandish comments by saying 'conspiracy theorists think...' as if that somehow distanced him from the lunacy of the words he was about to utter. Don't even start me on Area 51, UFOs and 9/11. We spent a lot of time laughing.

However, at 9am on a very hot Wednesday at the end of April 2016, we weren't laughing. Sean and I sat down in a meeting room we had hired for the day at the Imperial, with a large pot of coffee and the lengthy missive that Madame Dupont had sent me about the issues we faced with our intended business model.

The biggest issue we faced was around depot managers' ability to set prices as they saw fit to compete with the local market. This was a cornerstone of the UK success in that the price in say, Salisbury, may be higher than in Croydon simply because there were stronger competitors in Croydon to deal with. If the pricing was set on a nationwide basis by someone behind a large desk in London with a marketing degree, we could easily be too cheap in Salisbury and too expensive in Croydon. The best way to get the highest sales overall, at the highest margin possible, is to let the local managers set the price. Paying managers a share of the monthly profits is a very good way to ensure that they don't do stupid prices for the sake of it. This flew in the face of French values that decreed that everything should be fair, transparent and – ideally – dictated by the government.

Madame Dupont pointed out that there were two official sale periods in France each year in the retail market, both set by the government. One was in January/February, and the other was in June/July. These were the only times a company could apply discounts to products. A company still couldn't sell below cost though, even in a sale period. The logic behind this was to stop large companies entering a market and destroying local businesses with aggressive short-term pricing strategies. Trade companies such as ours were not bound by the discount diktat, as they would not normally be looking to the retail sector for sales, but we were bound by the transparency and fairness agenda that controlled our sector, and we were unable to sell below cost. Our issue was that because builders didn't buy kitchens in France, there wasn't really a set of rules that catered directly for a company that decided it wanted to try, and Madame Dupont was *extremely* good at pointing out that pretty much anything we did with discounts was going to break some law or other.

Another area of concern was in the way that a depot dealt with damaged products. In the UK, a manager would just write the product off against the margin and put it in the bin. Again, the policy of paying managers a share of the profits meant that they would only do this as a last resort after trying to sell it off cheaply first. This practice in our new business, while not illegal, was my first exposure to the French government's underlying primary objective – that of tax collection. If one of the many balaclava-clad heavies that could land at any time discovered a product write-off, they would conclude that we had actually sold this on a cash basis to avoid paying the tax on the sale, and would then charge us the tax that we would have made on that sale if it had gone through the books. The only way around this was if a government appointed bailiff came to our business establishment and witnessed the disposal of the product. They would then stamp our document with their official mark and disappear. This would be fine, if they didn't charge us two hundred euros for the pleasure each time they visited.

After a couple of hours staring at Madame Dupont's missive of doom, Sean and I needed a plan to start to deal with it. I was mindful of Didier telling me that there was 'always a way in France', and it was up to us to find it.

Sean said, 'Why don't I go and set up trade accounts in a few suppliers, including Cuisinex, and start to find out about how the discount structure works on a daily basis?'

That was good idea. I checked with Henri that we could use his home address as our pretend head office for the purposes of opening the accounts and off Sean went. I was going to spend my time getting kitchen prices from some different suppliers to see what that told us. We were going to re-group at 6.30pm at our newly designated 'Head Office' – McGuires, next door.

18

I set off on what transpired to be a frustrating day in kitchen studios trying to get prices. Firstly, trying to get somebody's attention was nigh on impossible. What few staff there were would do almost anything to avoid any eye contact with me. Whilst I usually received a distant 'bonjour' as I entered the establishment, by the time I had walked to where I thought I heard the voice come from, there was no-one. I could sometimes hear some scuffling from a particular direction, but by the time I had got there, again no-one. I decided that each showroom was designed to give salespeople many escape routes to get from A to B without ever being spotted by the enemy. Getting service in these places was more than a one-man job; I needed stooges at three points around the showroom to bounce the unwitting salesperson around the studio and into my grasp in the cleverly identified cul-de-sac of kitchen displays that I had discovered.

Eventually, I managed to trap a victim. Having explained that I needed a new kitchen fairly quickly and that I would like to sit down with a designer and my measurements to work out a price, the unlucky soul I had bagged cracked a small smile.

'I'm sorry sir,' he said, 'there are no designers in today.'

I said, 'What about you, can't you do it?'

To which he replied that he wasn't a designer, he was just here to make appointments for said designer.

'OK,' said I, 'Can I make an appointment please?'

'Of course, sir, please come with me.'

I went across to his little work station, upon which sat a computer screen that looked suspiciously to me as if it was in the middle of a kitchen plan being created, but what did I know. He said, 'Can you come in on Tuesday May 17th at 7pm?'

I said, 'That's more than two weeks away!'

To which he just said, 'Yes.'

I asked if he could send someone around to my house any

sooner and he said that they would only come to our house after we had agreed the plan and paid a five-hundred-euro deposit. And even then, only to make sure the design fitted.

I decided that it was going to be life-sapping to entertain this young man any further and was just walking out when I noticed the hanging sign saying that for every base unit purchased, you could get a wall unit of equivalent value for just one euro. I asked if that was a sale, given that we weren't in a sale period, to which he replied, 'It's not a sale, it's a promotion.' I didn't even bother challenging this, my sanity depended on it.

On one of my other visits that day, I discovered the tactic that the French government employ to try to deter people using cash in hand as a way to get a cheaper fitting price from their own builder. It transpired that if you buy your kitchen on a supply-only basis, you pay the current rate of VAT, around 20 per cent. If, however, you buy the kitchen on a supply and fit basis, you can buy the kitchen and the fitting from the kitchen studio at a much lower rate of tax for the whole transaction, usually around five or six per cent. This was another blow. It looked like our customers couldn't get a look in within this regime. The studios were only allowed to use bona fide tax-registered builders to make sure the government didn't miss out on any tax cents.

19

I arrived at McGuires at 6.30pm to find that Sean was already there and had ordered the drinks. It was a very hot day even though it was still only April, so the cold beer before me was most welcome. I gave Sean a quick run through of my day's events, the net result of which being absolutely nothing. Well, I suppose the fact that it appeared almost impossible to actually buy a kitchen in France meant that if we could find a way through the forest of problems before us, we should have a fair chance of success. That seemed quite a way off at the time though.

Sean told me about his day. In essence, it was a similar tale to mine, with supplier after supplier refusing to deal with him. Indeed, in a few, he couldn't even get through the front door without having the correct credentials. He did end up being more successful than I had been though, by calling on one of the recently appointed managers who, even though he hadn't yet started, was happy to help him.

Of the six managers we had already appointed, two were coming directly from companies that sold products to builders, and the other four had experience from this sector previously in their careers. All our new managers had told a similar story about how new customers were recruited, and it sounded almost unbelievable in that potential customers had to almost *apply* to be granted customer status. This was the reason that Sean wanted to test it himself. Surely it couldn't be *that* difficult. It turned out that it could... unless you had contacts.

Once Sean had called Stephane, a recent recruit who had been placed on gardening leave as soon as he had resigned, things became much, much easier. Stephane was coming from a plumbing and heating merchant, and as soon as Sean had Stephane by his side he was welcomed with open arms into that particular plumbing merchant which, just three hours earlier, wouldn't even let him through the front door.

Once inside, Sean was able to get an account application form. This was quite a lengthy document requiring several different registration numbers and proofs of ID. It was clear that we weren't going to be able to just use Henri's address to get an account open.

With Stephane by his side, Sean was able to chat to customers that were waiting to be served, and a story of a murky, intangible pricing structure started to emerge. Far from the clear and transparent system that Madame Dupont outlined, it seemed that, on a daily basis, things were far more opaque. The entry level discount was ten per cent. Everybody got this, to the point where you would wonder why they bothered with it. After that, further reductions were calculated retrospectively at the end of each month and a *rebate* based on spend that month was awarded. Even that wasn't cast in stone though, as the rebate level seemed to go up and down randomly to the point where none of the customers that Sean spoke to could actually tell him what price they would end up paying for today's purchases; it seemed to be all down to trust.

One observation Sean had made about the customers he had spoken to that day, was that none of them seemed in any hurry. He compared it to life in the UK depots where it is quite frenetic, with builders screaming to just get in, get their stuff and go. One of the customers remarked that he chose this particular merchant because the coffee was better than the others. Sean couldn't decide whether he was being serious or not, but with the amount of time these customers were spending at the trade counter, coffee quality was certainly going to be a consideration. The whole purchasing process seemed to be some kind of secret society, and Sean left the merchant feeling that there were still some large drivers within this process that he had overlooked.

Over our Chicken Tikka Masala that evening, we formed a plan for the next few days. Sean was going to speak to the UK computer team. We knew that the system they used to manage the depots already existed in French, but there would be a couple of weeks of adaptations to make it perfect for us. Similarly, the kitchen design programme was from a global company and also already existed in French, but, like the sales system, needed tweaking. As we didn't yet have our IT manager on board, Sean would take the lead on this for now.

While Sean was tackling the mysteries of hardware, software, uploads and downloads, I was going to have a relatively easy day driving around industrial estates in Paris, choosing some warehouses for us to rent. It would be a pleasant day out after the frustrations of today.

20

I have always used the same approach when I am looking for warehouse units to rent. Firstly, I buy a large street map of the town, but it must be the sort that opens right out, rather than a stapled book. This gives me perspective. Next, I use any means available to mark on the map all of our competitors and businesses that tradesman are likely to go to on a daily basis. This used to be the *Yellow Pages*, but life is not that simple any more.

Once I had done this, it was usually very easy to identify the trade hotspots in a town. Next, simply drive around those hotspots and find suitable units that are advertised as 'To Let'. By suitable, I mean that it has a car park for our customers, space for our trucks to unload, a large shutter door to get fork-lift trucks in and out, and hopefully some passing traffic to appeal to with our signage. If we were very lucky, there would be a burger van nearby as well. This is not because of my penchant for burgers, but more because these businesses are, by their very nature, mobile, and if they are in a particular location, it is because there is enough passing trade to justify it being there, and this is good information. Once the unit had been identified as suitable from the outside, I just needed a few minutes inside to check that it would be possible to trade from; this mainly meant not too much office space and with a high enough roof for the racking to fit.

My map exercise and previous drives around Paris had already pinpointed some trade hotspots in Paris. Aubervilliers to the north east of town and Nanterre to the north west were slam-dunks. Both had plenty of traffic and merchants squeezed into quite small areas. Being a new business to France, I wanted to get highly visible units for the first tranche of depots to give them the best chance possible.

It didn't take long in Aubervilliers to find a few 'To Let' signs on buildings that looked promising. I called the number on the first board.

'Hello, I'm in interested in a property you are renting out on Boulevard François Mitterrand.'

'Yes sir, which company are you from please?'

'I'm from a British company that is looking to set up in France.'

'Mmmm... OK, Monsieur Cosyn, who looks after that building, isn't here right now.'

'That's OK, could you just email me the details please?'

'Sorry sir, you need to speak to Monsieur Cosyn.'

'When will he be in?'

'Tomorrow sir.'

'Is there nobody else there that can help me out now?'

'No sir.'

'OK, please get him to call me then.'

'Certainly sir.'

Not to be put off by this complete lack of helpfulness, I called the next one, and had much the same story about having to speak to one specific person, but this time, my luck had changed and the lady that I needed was actually available.

'Hello, I'd like to get some details on a property you are renting out in Aubervilliers.'

'Which one sir?'

'The one next to the roundabout by McDonalds.'

'Ah, sorry sir, that one has already been let.'

'Oh, OK, not to worry, could you send me the details of every unit of around one thousand square metres that you have available in Aubervilliers and Nanterre please?'

'I have one in Ivry-sur-Seine that you might like.'

'That's nowhere near Aubervilliers or Nanterre.'

'I know, OK, I'll have a dig around and send you a couple of things.'

'When will you send them, please?'

'Tomorrow sir.'

'Why not today?'

'The person that sends out the details isn't in today.'

21

Back at Head Office that night, Sean told me a story of being passed from pillar to post with the IT guys, with no-one, either in the UK or France really wanting to help. He did finally secure a meeting with the point-of-sale system people in Paris, but that was for two weeks' time. Regarding the design software, he was waiting for a few call backs, but they were all based in Lille anyway.

When I recounted my tale of woe regarding the warehouses, Sean wasn't surprised; he was having a similar struggle trying to find a flat to rent. In addition to the issues that I was facing in just trying to get some details from agents, he had the additional burden of having to prepare a dossier on *himself* before letting agents would even speak to him. This covered things like the number of people to be in the flat, employment status, income, pets, smoking habits and things like that.

When I asked Sean if he had any other news from today, he said, 'Oh yes, I almost forgot, Stephane and one of the other managers have decided not to join us after all.'

22

After I had wiped all the beer that I had just spat out from off my clothes and the pub table, I said, 'What? Why? How? What did you do to that man when you saw him? Did you start talking about those damn Moon landings again?'

Sean looked a little flustered and said, 'No... well maybe a bit,'

He said that it was two different stories. When Stephane had taken Sean into the business he used to work in to talk to customers, the other staff had convinced Stephane that he had made a mistake by leaving. The other one cited 'personal reasons', and France's privacy laws forbade Sean from digging any deeper after that.

The reasons didn't really matter; we had gone two steps back today and we needed to take drastic action on the recruitment front to get back on track. I called Didier and we arranged to meet at the Imperial first thing in the morning. I called Henri as well; it was time we started deciding on what products we wanted to sell. That done, Sean and I continued our evening discussing most serious matters, such as which was the best band from The Jam, The Clash and The Stranglers. Sean was making a good case for it being The Stranglers, but he was wrong. It was The Jam. End of.

23

To be fair to Didier, he was making tremendous progress lining up interviews for the remaining positions that we needed to fill, notwithstanding that we probably now needed to over recruit to allow for the multitude of resignations I would be faced with as soon as they had met Sean!

We had at least one person to interview for every support position we needed to fill, and about 15 people to interview for the depot managers' positions. The French interview process is much more formulaic and lengthier than my attention span can deal with, so I asked Didier to conduct the first interviews for the support staff alone, and I would do a second, more 'British' interview after that to assess whether I thought these people would fit into our business. Sean decided that he wanted to be a part of all the interviews for the managers' positions. Didier mentioned that he was getting a lot of people applying from the area around Hauts-de-France region, and Lille in particular. He said that there was more unemployment in that area compared to Paris, and that people were generally cheaper to recruit. This tied in with a thought that had been developing in my head for a while now, in that the Lille area would be a good place to set up our head office and a few depots.

Didier had interviews lined up for the rest of that day and Monday in an office he had rented for a few months near Gare du Nord. He was also meeting a supplier of lease cars and a payroll provider, so he disappeared, and we started discussing product with Henri.

My overriding plan with the business was to set it up exactly like the UK business and then adapt it as we went along. I believed that if I had adapted it before we opened and it didn't work, we would never have known if it was the adaptations that had caused the failure. I convinced myself by concentrating on McDonalds, who operated in a very similar way in France to the core US business, even though when they were setting it up, you can bet your bottom dollar that there were many advisors telling them that they should be selling baguettes and Bordeaux, rather than burgers and milkshakes.

In keeping with my plan, I wanted to start with the same secondary product groups that the UK sold; this included window blinds, flooring, hand tools and the associated fixings and accessories for these products. For the kitchens, we needed sinks, taps and appliances. The reason for selling complementary products at all was that builders in the UK buy those items much more frequently than they buy an expensive kitchen, so by selling very cheap 'commodity products', we give ourselves an opportunity to earn the builder's trust, develop a relationship, and get a chance of explaining our model to him and how he can make some good money fitting kitchens. It didn't matter that we made little or no margin on the commodity products; it could almost be viewed as a marketing expense.

Henri had spent time looking at the UK catalogue and had already prepared some notes. He said that the window blind market was very different in the UK and he advised against selling them. He said that the flooring market was good for us, and that a lot of the UK flooring product would be fine in France. While some of the UK ancillary products like fixings and mastics would function perfectly well, the English labelling precluded our selling them.

Henri's primary concern with the window blind market was that in the UK the 80/20 rule applied in terms of range, where 80% of your sales normally come from 20% of your products, whereas the French market was much more fragmented with specialists tending to serve this market rather than generalists like us. It was a good point; Sean and I had noticed that the blinds we had seen for sale were very ornate and vast in terms of styles and sizes. However, I wanted to stick to my guns and asked Henri to find us a middle ground range between the made to measure blinds that were available at specialists and the very cheap entry level ones that we had seen on shelves in DIY stores, the level of dust consistently on top of said blinds being a good clue as to how frequently they were being purchased. Henri grumped a bit but agreed.

With kitchen products, it was an easier discussion. Henri knew this market well, so I was happy for him to determine the locally purchased products that we sold to help us sell the kitchen. We couldn't use very many of the UK appliances, due to plugs being on a lot of products. Items like ovens, hobs and hoods don't usually have plugs on, but the next issue was that of brand. The brands that were popular in the UK were not necessarily the brands that the French preferred, so we decided to start from scratch on appliances, as well as sinks and taps, where again, different regulations and brand preference meant that the UK range wasn't going to work.

Henri then asked a very simple question. 'When I've bought all of this stuff, where am I going to put it?'

This was a very good question. In Florida, we had asked the suppliers to deliver to every depot, every week, and whilst this looked good on paper, at depot level, having so many deliveries each week became problematic and the differing types of dispatch notes from each supplier caused serious problems loading the stock onto the system, which created stock management problems and therefore stock losses.

This time around, I was either going to rent a large unit to use as a distribution centre or use third party logistics to manage it for us. Third party logistics, or 3PL as they are known, is an expensive way to manage your stock as you are paying for every space on every rack you use, every day, as well as the transport from the warehouse to the depots, but the flexibility it affords is a tremendous advantage.

Henri was in favour of using 3PL, and he had a contact in Paris that could help us. This contact had provided Henri's logistics when he worked in the clothing company in the late '70s. At least that was one less thing to think about.

Regarding marketing, I wanted it to look exactly like the UK literature and branding. We were going to trade as 'Eastney Intérieurs' in France, despite everyone saying that it didn't mean anything in France. My response to that was always that it didn't mean anything in England either. I believed that French people could type it into their search engine and at least see the size of the UK business to give our test some credibility.

For the catalogues and price lists, again, I wanted corporate uniformity. This meant having a kitchen catalogue that was presented in landscape form. Henri opened a large carrier bag he had by his side and pulled out what must have been 50 kitchen catalogues from other French suppliers, and they were all, without exception, in portrait format. Henri said, 'Landscape format is viewed as Italian in France, so we should stick to what French people are used to.'

I explained that landscape format presented the average kitchen photograph better than portrait, so we would be sticking to landscape. After more grumping while stuffing his 50 catalogues back into his carrier bag, we agreed that there was enough for Henri to be getting on with for now, and that we would re-group the following week.

24

At about 2pm that day, I received a call from Monsieur Cosyn from the property agency I had called the day previously. He informed me that the building I was interested in was not available anymore, but he had another one just like it, and he could meet me there on Monday to look at it. I agreed to this, mainly because I had no other choices at that stage, and at least a face-to-face meeting with an agent might give me a better understanding of how the market operated in France. In the UK, I could call three or four different agents in the morning and have, probably, 50 different flyers emailed to me by that afternoon. I could then quickly drive past them all, eliminate 45 of them instantly, and then plan to go in to the five possible options. It seemed like France didn't operate like that at all. No, not at all.

25

Sean and I had got to the unit in Aubervilliers about 20 minutes ahead of our meeting with Monsieur Cosyn on the Monday, and it took us a full ten seconds to exclude this particular building on the grounds that it didn't have a floor level warehouse door, but instead had dock height doors where large trucks could back straight up to it and the forklift could stay inside the warehouse while unloading, driving straight into the truck if required. This was no good for us; our customers would want to drive into our buildings on occasions to load up.

Monsieur Cosyn was about ten minutes late for our meeting, but felt no need to apologise for, or even explain his late arrival. His car was a Peugeot that had certainly been around the Arc de Triomphe a few times judging by the number of dents and scratches on it. He was a portly man, with a face that looked like it had enjoyed quite a few cheese and wine parties over the years.

After the introductions, Monsieur Cosyn started his presentation. First, he gave us the dossier on this particular building, in itself a 12-page document. He then proceeded to walk us around the perimeter of the entire building, pointing out doors and windows. Then, when we finally got inside, we were led around every nook and cranny of this staggeringly boring building. Every cupboard was opened and light switch examined. This tour took about 40 minutes, and I was losing the will to live by the end of it. However, I smiled sweetly and asked if he had anything else for us to look at as there was another one of his agency's boards a little way down the road. He said that the boards were irrelevant as they usually only put them up when they had leased the unit, as a form of advertising. On the occasions where there was a board up on a unit that was actually available, it would be on a building that had been empty for a considerable while with no interest. Us, as mere customers though, had no idea which category any particular boarded building fell into. When I explained this dilemma to Monsieur Cosyn, he just shrugged his shoulders and changed the subject.

26

It was now mid-May, and we had been making good progress in all camps. We had agreed terms with all the support staff we needed, which was great because we were currently spending a small fortune on agency staff to cover the bases in the short term.

Didier had used a translation agency to convert all the UK staff handbooks, safety manuals, contracts and other important documents into French. Whilst the company needed to be compliant in France first and foremost, it also needed to stick to the UK company's values and culture. The translation work itself was costing us a packet, but there was no way around it. Didier was now going through the translated documents, making the adjustments needed for it to be a legally compliant French business. He had also done a deal with a car leasing company, outsourced payroll, and was currently in the middle of interviewing for the last of the managers we needed with Sean. Didier was definitely earning his keep.

Henri had worked wonders with the product range and marketing, albeit again with a lot of help from agency staff. The only critique I had was that the window blind range he recommended looked a bit narrow to me, so I asked him to treble it in terms of different products. He stared at me like I had just escaped from the local asylum and said, 'That's madness.'

To which I replied that he may well be correct, but the optics needed to be right. We were going to be the new kids on the block and we needed to be seen as doing the job properly. Having a wide range of products available to our customer was a very good way of being seen to be serious, even if, as Henri strongly believed, we would never sell a lot of it.

The logistics company had been assigned and they were now ready and waiting for our inbound deliveries.

The catalogues and price lists were ready to be sent to the printers. We had finally got to the bottom of the discount and pricing issue. It was all about terminology, but at no point did any of our French 'experts' point that out to us; we had to work it out for ourselves. It turned out to be a lightbulb moment that Sean and I had in McGuires one evening.

We were aware of the French rebate system for companies that sold to the trade, so we wondered if we could just call our 'discount' a 'rebate', and rather than apply it retrospectively at the end of each month, simply apply it to the invoice at the point of sale.

I called Madame Dupont the next day with this question, and she said that she would investigate. Later, she called back and said that she couldn't find any reason why we couldn't do that and would confirm it in writing. The nebulous area of how much rebate each customer got and who decided this amount was also fairly straightforward in the end. The same regulation that governed the unpredictable retrospective rebates in the plumbing merchant Sean visited, allowed us to set our prices on the day by the local manager. Again though, had I not asked this specific and direct question of Madame Dupont, I don't get the sense that she would ever have offered the information. So, in a similar way that the first person I spoke to in a kitchen studio said, 'It's not a sale, it's a promotion,' we just needed to change one word for another so that when the French regulation militia came storming the building, they would leave empty handed.

Regarding property, I had signed off seven buildings: four in Paris, two around Lille and one in Meaux, which was about an hour's drive to the west of Paris. There had proven to be no easy solution to dealing with the property agents; it was another French game. Each time I contacted one, they would send me one or two choices. These would always be the stuff they had been trying to unload for eons and were desperate to shift. It would then take five or six more conversations before I got any of the good properties that the agent was always sitting on, and only then if I was dutifully respectful and observed all of the protocols. This usually meant smiling sweetly, pretending to be interested in all the light switches, and waxing lyrical over the efforts they had put into the dossier for each building. It was a painful, one by one, process but it was manageable.

We were going to make our head office in Lille, and one of the buildings we had agreed terms on there had an annexe to one side of about 700 square metres. Having our base in Lille meant that we could get people across quite easily from London via the Eurostar, and it was easily driveable from Calais as well. The fact that people were cheaper to recruit in Lille was an additional bonus. This shift in focus, at least in terms of support functions, meant that we needed another hotel to call 'home'. Having tried a few places, we settled on the Crest International, largely because we could negotiate the underground car park easier than all the others, but it was also only a short walk to the main square from there, with all the pavement bars, shops and character of the wonderful city that Lille is.

We were already fitting out four of the depots, including the one at Seclin in southern Lille, where we were to establish our head office. Whilst it was good to see people with hammers and saws in the buildings, I couldn't help thinking that they could *surely* work a bit faster than *that*!

Systems were proving a bit of an issue. We knew that both the sales system and the design system needed 'a bit of tweaking', but what we didn't know was that both sets of 'tweaking' were going to take about three months and, again, cost a small fortune. The money was an irritation, but the delay meant that we would only get our systems a matter of weeks before we opened, and until we had them, we couldn't do any training, or dispatch any products to the depots. It was still possible, but it was cutting it very fine.

In terms of the new team starting, Claude, our finance director, was due to start on Monday, and the heads of IT, property and credit control were starting the week after. This meant that I could hold my first weekly 'Executive' meeting in the Crest at Lille, on Monday 27th June. I was looking forward to it.

The meeting was given a different perspective though, when I spoke to Bernard who said that he'd like to come across for that meeting, see a few of the new depots and have dinner with the team. Unfortunately, Bernard couldn't do the 27th, so he would come over the week before on the 20th. Before I could say 'but I won't have everybody by then', he'd gone.

27

Arranging a visit from Bernard was quite a challenge. He didn't have a secretary in the true sense of the word. Well, there was a lady in London called Imogen that tried to keep up with him, but it was a hopeless and thankless task. He had no laptop, computer or email account; his diary was kept in the breast pocket of his jacket and, between that and his ancient mobile phone, his entire life was managed. Once he had decided that he was going to be in a certain place on a certain day, it was up to the local operative – in this case, me – to make all the arrangements, including flights, hotels, restaurants, depot visits and meetings, of which there should never be too many.

I knew that Bernard had taken many holidays in the south of France in the past, as he had frequently mentioned the areas of Toulon and Antibes with fondness and often remarked about the quality of the food in those areas. This was a distinct worry for me; my experience of French food up to this point was a very good Indian restaurant near the Imperial and a few bistros and restaurants around Paris that were adequate, but certainly no more than that. It seemed that there was a whole world of French dining perfection somewhere out there that was, thus far, eluding me.

I had one week to arrange a visit, and this became my focal point for the next few days. I called the three department managers that weren't due to have started until the week after his visit and begged them to come in for the meeting and the dinner. Thankfully, they all agreed. They said it would be nice to meet the *grand chef* so soon in their careers with us, and I said that I agreed. There was nothing to be gained by sharing my nervousness at this point.

I knew the pilot of Bernard's plane fairly well. Frank Baines was an ex-RAF pilot who, after serving his country for 18 years, decided to leave the armed forces and set up his own business. Initially, he acted as an agent, connecting passengers and charter flight companies together. After a couple of years of this, he decided to take the plunge and borrow the money to lease a small plane for two years. He currently had a Cessna Citation and had three or four regular customers, one of whom was Bernard. He also still acted as an intermediary for other clients who required different aircraft. He said that while he was never going to get rich doing the job he did, it kept the wolf from the door, and he actually really enjoyed it.

When arranging private flights for Bernard, large airports were to be avoided if at all possible. The last thing I wanted was Bernard at Lille-Lesquin Airport having to wait for shuttle cars to arrive at his plane, being shepherded through airport security and then being interrogated by all and sundry on his way through to meet me.

I spoke to Frank, and it turned out that even though there are many small airfields around Lille, only one has the facilities to receive international arrivals. This airfield was in Merville, about one hour's drive from Lille, so I got in my car to see how it might work logistically. I knew that Bernard would much prefer to sit in the back of a car for an hour than spend 20 minutes fighting his way through a large and impersonal airport

Merville looked good from the outside. Chain link fencing meant that you could see the whole airfield from the car park, and it was small enough that the plane could taxi right up to the terminal. When I say terminal, I mean a building about ten metres by 20 metres with glass on three sides, meaning you could see right through to the runway from the outside.

The types of aircraft dotted around led me to think that this airfield was predominantly used for recreational purposes. I spoke to the solitary individual inside the terminal, and he informed me that when they are expecting an international arrival, they ship a passport official in from Lille-Lesquin just for that passenger. It looked like it would be about three minutes between Bernard exiting his plane to being safely in the back of my car. This was looking good.

Next thing to sort out was the hotel. I had planned to use the

Crest but it wasn't really Bernard's sort of place. He disliked 'boxy, corporate dormitories' as he called them, and whilst the Crest was a wonderful hotel in many regards, it did lack a bit of character or soul. There is another decent quality hotel in Lille, called Le Couvent. This hotel was originally built in the 15th century, and whilst it had been expanded over the centuries, it retained many original features and most definitely had the character that I was looking for. There was on street parking right outside as well. I smelled a good visit ahead of me.

With just the dinner to sort out for the housekeeping element of the visit, Sean and I had a few days to test some restaurants before deciding where to take him. Hopefully, we would find some of the French *je ne sais quoi* in food form that was supposed to be out there somewhere.

We bunkered in at the Couvent for the whole of that week. It was a good way to get to know a few people there so that when we arrived with Bernard, we would at least be recognised and, hopefully, served quickly. This restricted the choice of restaurant to those that we could walk to from that hotel. Whilst it is possible to order taxis in France, it is not an easy or particularly pleasant experience. Another irritation with French taxis is the fact that the driver will put his meter on at the time he gets the job allocated, so you can easily get into a French taxi to find that it already has 20 or 30 euros on the meter depending on how far the driver has driven to pick you up. This was not a problem though, Lille is a beautiful city, and the 'old town' was a 15-minute walk from the hotel, within which were many shops, bars and restaurants. If nothing else, I thought that Bernard would enjoy the surroundings here.

I decided to invite some of the new recruits out to dinner over the nights we were in the Couvent to get to know them a bit better, Whilst, on the food front, it may even be that one of them knew of the culinary excellence that I was searching for.

The first dinner we had on our rapid-fire tasting tour of Lille was with finance director Claude, and Yasmine Blanchet our new head of IT and systems. The four of us were going to wander into the old town after an aperitif in the bar at the Couvent first. I had met Yasmine and Claude once, but Sean had not, so we had an hour or so at the hotel to start to get to know each other.

Of the four of us, Claude was the most vocal and Yasmine was by some margin the least. She was coming to us from a pharmaceutical company in Lyon. Her husband needed to transfer to the north of France for his work, and they decided that rather than him commute weekly, Yasmine would move north as well. She had controlled a team of ten people in her previous employment but didn't strike me as a natural leader. I suppose I needed to see her in her working environment to get a better sense of that though.

Claude was good company. He told us about his wife, Fleur, his two children, Alice and Raphael, and his dog, Booboo. I had a dog as well, so we had some common ground. It was too soon to ascertain the sorts of relationships they all had, but if time spent talking about them was a measure of love, then Booboo was top of the pile.

We walked to a restaurant that Claude had suggested. It had received great reviews on the internet, and he had been there before with his wife. Unfortunately, it was one of those occasions where I knew the second we arrived that it wasn't going to be right for us and then had to almost waste an evening sitting there. It was just too big and impersonal to be of any use for Bernard's visit. It was, though, an opportunity to try out some different food and maybe unlock the mystery of French cuisine.

I deliberately ordered last so I could choose something that no-one else had, and ended up with a pork chop in some creamy mustard sauce as my reward. I think that mine looked the best of the four when it arrived, with Yasmine's looking the worst; she had ordered a seafood dish called bouillabaisse, which looked to me like the remnants from a fishmonger's floor.

Sean and Yasmine were chatting about the progress that was being made, or rather the lack of it, on all of our systems requirements. The thing that had appealed to me about Yasmine when I met her was that she didn't talk in jargon or initials, she was able to talk me through her career without drifting into technical references. Listening to her talking to Sean though, made me wonder a bit about her. Sean was by no means an expert in this area, his basic knowledge having been gained by no more than his involvement in this programme to date, but he knew enough to have a level of conversation that was certainly above my head.

When Sean was giving Yasmine a brief summary of our progress, she didn't ask any questions; well, not any that I couldn't have asked myself anyway. It struck me as slightly odd that our head of IT wasn't slightly more inquisitive regarding the developments in her area of expertise. On a couple of occasions, I even thought I caught her changing the subject, but I may have been being over-sensitive.

Overall, it was a good evening. I gently advised that they be careful what they said at our up-coming meeting, so that they could hopefully avoid saying anything contentious. The conversation that evening flowed well and I felt we had common ground. Sean entertained the table with his Connery impression, which always went down well, and Claude, for his part, left me feeling at the end of the evening like I knew Booboo personally.

28

On the Wednesday of that week, I was able to muster Didier, Henri, our new property manager Camille Boucher, and our new credit controller, Gabrielle Dubois for dinner. Including Sean and I, the six of us had booked a table at a small family run restaurant recommended by Henri, the Grille de Lille.

As soon as we walked into this place it felt right. We were welcomed by a man who turned out to be the owner and was wearing his chef's whites, and he showed us to our table. We were offered an aperitif and given some menus very promptly. The ambience in here was excellent. There was a grill in the corner where the owner was already placing big slabs of beef for another table, and the gentle serenade of Charles Aznavour's *La Bohème* in the background made it just perfect.

However, when I picked up the laminated menu to read it, I thought that I must have been given only a part of it. I looked at the back, and that was blank, and on the front were just seven options, one chicken, one lamb and five beef. There were no appetisers, no side dishes or vegetables, and no deserts. Just seven cuts of meat.

Exercising my right as a Brit abroad to ask questions about a menu, I enquired of the young lady that was taking our order regarding the lack of choices available. She told us that this restaurant had been here over 50 years and the current owner was the son of the founder. She was the owner's daughter, and her brother was the only other person working tonight, who was serving some drinks. She said that the restaurant was 'all about the meat' and that appetizers and side dishes merely acted as a distraction to the chef who was trying to make each meal perfect. To that end, each meal was served with a jacket potato and a side salad, and there was a cheeseboard available afterwards for those that desired it. We all ordered our meal, and the lady scurried away to the next table. Looking around, there were probably 12 or 13 tables, and only two were empty, so the chef's formula for success seemed to be working.

The meal took about 30 minutes to arrive, but that didn't matter on this occasion; it gave us a chance to have a chat and Didier, with his background in interrogation, was doing a good job of getting Camille and Gabrielle involved in the conversation.

Camille was coming to us from an industrial estate agent, much like the companies that I was dealing with to find the properties we had found so far. She also managed some properties for investors and was used to co-ordinating tradespeople on refurbishment work. This was great news for me; I had been organising people on a very ad-hoc basis so far, and whilst we had made a start, it wasn't going very quickly and I hoped Camille could grab it and put some energy into it.

Gabrielle was a very lively lady, very enthusiastic about joining us, and was particularly excited to hear that I had arranged for her to travel to the UK to work with the credit control team there for a couple of weeks. We were quite strict about debt collection, and I wanted to make sure we had the same disciplines in France.

When our meal arrived, I must admit to being a little disappointed. It wasn't that my choice of steak was presented poorly, it was just that I had expected something a little more spectacular from a restaurant that prides itself on being 'all about the meat'. It tasted alright though, and I thought that Bernard would be OK here; it was just about quirky enough. However, it appeared that my quest to find the renowned *haute cuisine* would have to wait another day.

Talking to Sean in the Couvent bar after dinner that night, I felt we had made real progress, the team seemed good. We both had some reservations about Yasmine, the IT manager, but that could wait a while. We had found some properties and were fitting them out, we had product to look at and marketing products to scrutinise. Better than all that though, we had found a decent airport, hotel and restaurant for Bernard's visit, which was now just a few days away.

We decided that the best thing to do with Bernard was to have the meeting with the department heads in the Couvent straight after he landed at about 3pm. We would all give him an update on our respective departments, even though some of these people hadn't even started with us yet. It would give Bernard a sense of who the new recruits were. We would then have drinks in the hotel before walking to the Grille de Lille for dinner. The next day, we would drive him around some of the properties, in both Lille and down in Paris, before dropping him off at Le Bourget Airport in Paris to fly back. This airport was far less controversial because Frank, his pilot, had told me that Bernard was familiar with it, so even if I got lost in that area, he could direct me in.

That was it, we were set for the visit.

29

On the Monday of Bernard's visit, he called me at about 8am saying that he was bringing the UK finance director, Fiona Harris, over with him. This didn't present a problem in itself, it just meant booking another hotel room and telling the restaurant. I did wonder why she was coming though; it was unusual for her to leave the warmth and creature comforts of her office in London.

As was always the case for me, I arrived at Merville Airport early, in this instance a full 90 minutes early. I had brought Sean along with me to collect them, so that if questions arose about the depot staff, Sean could answer them more fully than I could. We calculated that we had probably arrived at their destination airport before they had even arrived at their departure airport. No matter, there was a small café close by to grab a coffee.

Bang on time, we saw the Citation land and taxi to the terminal, and in less than five minutes our visitors were in my car and we were heading back to the Couvent.

'How was the flight, Bernard?'

'Fine.'

'It looks like the weather is being kind to us today.'

'Yes.'

I was sensing that the Bernard that had arrived was not necessarily the one I was hoping for. During the rather quiet drive back to Lille, Bernard asked what our agenda was over the coming day or so, and after I had told him, in as enthusiastic a tone as I could muster, he just said, *'Mmm...'*

Back at the hotel, the management team were all waiting in the meeting room I had booked. It was the first time I had seen them all together, and after I had given some basic introductions, Bernard and Fiona sat down, followed swiftly by Sean and myself. The French contingent, however, were still chatting and getting themselves coffee, oblivious to the impending bruising we were about to get, if my senses were anything to go by.

I said, 'Come on guys, let's get started,' and they all said, *'yes, no problem'* but then carried on getting their coffee anyway, as if it was utterly unimaginable that a meeting could begin until they had coffee in front of them. To add further frustration, the machine we had in the room made each cup individually and noisily; it seemed to take an eternity. I glanced at Bernard and he glanced back with a knowing smile. I just shook my head and stared despairingly at my notepad.

Eventually, the team settled down, got their pens and pads out, put their bags on the floor and stopped fidgeting, so I began. I said, 'Shall we all give a brief summary of what's been happening so far, Bernard?' to which he replied, 'Later. I want to start with budgets.' He then handed over to Fiona, who gave out a single A4 page to each of us a with a breakdown of what had been spent and already committed to date. It also showed some forecasts about where the overall costs were likely to end up based on our previous experience in Florida. It was looking like this project was going to cost about 40 per cent more than opening in the USA.

After Fiona had talked us through the numbers, the room went quiet. It wasn't worth trying to offer any defence, the numbers were all correct, but I had just been doing what I needed to do on a daily basis to get going. Oh, and not overlooking the fact that my finance director had started working for me all of six hours ago.

'So, what are you going to do about that then?' asked Bernard.

'Well, I'm going to have to see where I can save a bit, aren't I?'

'You're going to have to do quite a bit more than that I'm afraid; I want to see a 40 per cent reduction from this budget.'

'Oh...'

'Yes, oh...'

With that, Bernard got up, said that he would let us think about that for a while and went to leave the room. When he got to the door, he turned around and said cheerily, 'What time are we meeting at the bar?' I answered 6.30pm, to which he just said, 'Perfect, 6.30 then, looking forward to it.'

I, on the other hand, most definitely wasn't.

I glanced around the room at a group of recently recruited French department managers, looking at each other with faces that said, 'What on earth have we done?'

Sean made a jocular comment about them having just witnessed an approximate three on the Richter Scale, and that they should all consider themselves very lucky. This made them laugh, nervously I suspect.

After he had left the room, Fiona explained, almost apologetically, that she had received a call from Bernard on Friday asking for a brief summary of costs compared to Florida, which she had duly provided. Then, first thing this morning he called her again, telling her she was going to France with him today, so to pack a bag. She'd had to cancel meetings with external auditors, pension trustees and our bankers to visit France, but she knew Bernard wanted this sorted, so offered no resistance.

The extra costs were mainly down to the language barrier and social charges. Getting everything translated by external agencies and the extra work required on the systems was an open wound haemorrhaging cash. This work wasn't required in Florida, and the social charges in France being about 45 per cent compared to about 13 per cent in America also had a dramatic effect on the comparison. Fiona said that if you overlooked those two items, the rest of the costs were broadly in line. In fact, the shorter lease lengths in France made the overall commitment lower. She flagged the extra cost of the third-party logistics but said that it was the most sensible way to get going in her opinion.

At the bar that night, and throughout the meal at the restaurant, Bernard was charming and entertaining to the team, reserving any thinly veiled criticism for myself and Sean, and even then, in such a way that it is unlikely the French team picked up on it. The wine flowed freely and light-hearted stories were told of the tribulations and mistakes that we made setting up the UK and the American businesses.

After what must have been the fourth large Cognac following dinner, we left the restaurant and walked slowly back to the Couvent. Bernard was walking beside me, while Sean and the French contingent were all behind us, chatting outside the restaurant in a huddle, with most of them lighting up a cigarette. As I looked back at the circle of people all puffing away, it looked a bit like a new Pope had been elected.

Along the route back, Bernard said, 'Good bunch there, Peter, well done.'

I thanked him and said that it was early days, but so far, so good.

He then said, 'But you really do need to get a hold of the costs here.'

I said to him that I would do my best, to which he replied in a very matter-of-fact way, 'Yes, let's hope that's enough.'

30

Breakfast at the Couvent Hotel was quite a formal affair. It has a buffet in much the same way that most hotels do these days, this being a sign of 'progress' that I fundamentally dislike, but in the Couvent, it is still served in a five-star environment with five-star service. The fact that I only ever have a glass of juice and a coffee just means that the five-star price they charge for it sticks in the throat a bit.

Having arrived at the breakfast table ridiculously early as usual, Sean and I were discussing the best route to take Bernard and Fiona today. We had planned to get them to Le Bourget at about 3pm, which meant that we had to provide a lunch somewhere. This was another potential issue, in that sometimes he would want a sit-down lunch with a glass of wine, and sometimes the very same plan would be dismissed out of hand. Again, you never quite knew which way it would go. I had opted for a sandwich, given the previous night's excesses, and therefore our route had to get us to the best friterie that we knew of at around lunchtime, this being near a depot we had just leased close to Le Bourget Airport. Due to the timings, he would probably decide to go straight to the plane after his sandwich.

When Bernard arrived at the table, he sat down and ordered a large pot of coffee just for himself and said, 'What's the plan for today then?' I started telling him which depots we were going to and who we were going to meet along the way, when he said, 'Actually, I've decided that you getting the numbers in order is more important than that, so just take me back to Merville please and get on with finding those savings.' He called Frank and asked him to get to Merville Airfield as soon as he could, which was about 90 minutes time, so a bit of breakfast and an hour's drive back to Merville worked perfectly. Well, perfect for Bernard anyway, I wasn't quite so sure how Frank felt about it.

Having dropped them off at Merville without further incident, we waved them off and started the journey back to Lille. Sean was phoning the staff we were due to meet today, who had been polishing their car parks and warehouse floors for the impending visit, to tell them they could stand down. For my part, I left a message on Claude's phone to call me back; we needed to start to drill down into the numbers.

After a while of quiet contemplation driving through the agricultural lands of north-west France, as if from nowhere, Sean piped up, 'So, don't you think it odd, that with all of the footage there is of the planes crashing into the World Trade Center, both in terms of news crews and personal phone videos, that there is just one, very grainy CCTV film of the plane going into the Pentagon? I mean, it's just really, really unlikely, isn't it? You would expect that there would be far more cameras covering the land surrounding the Pentagon than the World Trade Center wouldn't you? Conspiracy theorists think...'

Mercifully, my phone rang. It was Claude calling me back. I asked him to meet us back at the Crest, the Couvent having served its purpose for the time being.

It's only a 20-minute walk from the Couvent to the Crest International, so by the time Sean and I got there, Claude was waiting for us, laptop open and poised. Fiona had already sent him the details that she had, but most of the other numbers he needed were either on scraps of paper in my wallet, hidden away in our emails somewhere, or for the most part, just floating around in Sean's or my head.

During this fragmented and clumsy debrief, Claude commented that this exercise was a bit like doing a jigsaw, but when you didn't know how many pieces there were or what the picture was. This was a fair comment. It took the rest of that day to transfer every detail that was number related from Sean and I across to Claude, but once done, it felt good that somebody now owned the numbers.

At about 7pm when we had finally finished, Claude closed his laptop and was just about to head off home. He said, 'Guys, I just wanted to let you know that these have been the most chaotic, crazy, unpredictable and fun first two days of any job I've ever had.' He said it with a smile on his face, and I got no sense that he was having second thoughts about joining us. It did, however, make me think that the rollercoaster ride that is working for Eastney Interiors might not sit comfortably with the traditional French balance that exists between work and home life, or how differing levels of hierarchy interact with each other. Only time would tell.

That night, Sean and I sat in an Indian restaurant we had found in Lille, near the Ramparts. It was in Rue de Gand, a road with pretty much nose to tail restaurants all the way along it, most of which were of the traditional French cuisine. The lack of variety in the range of food types available in France was becoming noticeable and frustrating.

Having relieved myself of the detail of the numbers, I felt somehow unburdened. Even though I knew they were still my problem, I felt more relaxed than in a long time. Claude said he would have some suggestions on the savings by Thursday, so until then at least, I could forget about them.

I suggested to Sean that it would be good to take as many people as we could muster back to the UK to visit the depots and the suppliers that provided the products. This would reinforce the culture message we wanted to get across and introduce them to some depot managers who were running fantastic businesses and earning significant bonuses. I wanted to give the French depot teams a sense of what could be achieved with hard work. We would take the support team as well, if for no other reason than to act as interpreters where needed. We would also take this opportunity to put some proper food in front of our new French friends.

I asked Sean to deal with logistics and arrangements in France, and I was going to sort out the plan in the UK. Sean asked whether I thought that this idea, whilst sounding great after a few glasses of wine, might actually prove quite challenging. I immediately dismissed this negative point of view and poured us another glass.

The rest of that evening was spent deliberating over whether Harry Enfield or Paul Whitehouse had introduced better comedy characters to us over the years. It was a tense and emotive discussion, but I think Harry won by a short head.

31

Thursday 27ᵗʰ June, 10am in a meeting room at the Crest International. I was with Sean waiting for Claude to arrive, slightly excited to find out how we were going to make the savings we needed. It was my first exposure to how Claude presented his work, and I was hoping that I would find it easy to understand.

When he arrived, and after he had sourced a coffee (obviously), he said, 'Did you see the spreadsheet I sent you both late last night?' to which I answered, 'No, I was rather hoping you would be able to talk me through it without a spreadsheet.'

This turned out not to be the case. 'OK don't worry,' he said, 'I've bought hard copies.' Not in any way discouraged by my slightly negative stance on this, he opened his briefcase, dived headlong into it and emerged, smiling triumphantly with a thick green folder for each of us.

32

Recipe:

Take one verbose accountant, add a large amount of data and a sprinkle of coffee. Bake on a depressingly low heat for two hours, or until your audience dies.

33

It was one of those times where I was always hopeful that when I turned a page, the bit I was waiting for was going to be there somewhere, only to be dashed each time by more detail about the number of years we should depreciate the racking over, or how French pension charges are calculated.

I was trying to be polite. For a start, Claude had clearly put an awful lot of work into this, and he was proud of the results, in that they were comprehensive and thorough. My worry was that if we didn't get to the juicy bit soon, I would be a pension statistic myself.

With as much diplomacy as I could muster, and on one of the rare moments that Claude paused for breath, I gently asked if he had actually come to any conclusions about the savings, and, if he had, could we do that bit now please, and then come back to the social charges ready reckoner later if needed.

He looked like someone had just told him that Booboo had died; he was utterly crestfallen. I think he viewed this presentation like a rendition of Elgar's *Pomp and Circumstance*, where the beauty of the piece is in the entire 25 minutes of the work. Unfortunately for Claude, I just wanted to get to the bit where everyone belts out *Land of Hope and Glory*.

Almost begrudgingly, he mumbled, 'If you turn to page 68, you will see that if we opened one fewer depot than planned, the capital saving would offset the translation charges. If we then take the building that we aren't trading from and use it to bring the logistics in-house, the reduced operational costs bring profitability forward by one year, but there is literally nothing we can do about social charges, short of having fewer people – you either want to trade in France, or you don't.'

I would like to be able to say at this point that Claude sat back proudly and allowed the warm glow of a job well done to gently wash over him, but this being Claude, he dived straight back to page 52 where there was a fascinating breakdown of intangible assets that he wanted to show me.

34

Now, in early July, our opening date was hurtling toward us, and I was mindful that we were entering the holiday season. Fortunately for me, the way that French holiday pay is accrued meant that my new recruits would be unlikely to desert me during August this year. Both Didier and Sean had warned me of the physical and psychological shutdown that occurs in the holiday season in France each year, but I was hopeful that we could muddle through this year at least.

We had now agreed terms on all ten of our buildings, including the one that would accommodate our head office in Lille, and the one that was now going to be our distribution centre. We had decided to use the one near Le Bourget that we were previously going to take Bernard to, as it was bigger than the others, and it had differing door types for the trucks to use. Its proximity to the A1 between Paris and Lille also made it ideal. The fit-outs were at varying stages, with a couple already finished and some not yet started. Whenever I went to a depot that had workers present, I was more often than not greeted by a group of fitters hanging around outside smoking cigarettes. It is fair to say that the level of work-rate that I was witnessing in France was not the same as I had been used to in the UK or Florida. That's not to say that they were lazy, the work seemed to get done; it's just that I never actually *saw* it being done. We had prioritised the Le Bourget building as we needed somewhere to put our stock fairly soon, but with no systems yet to receive it onto, it would have to be very manual for the time being. Whenever I called Yasmine about systems issues and delays, she always seemed to be waiting for someone in the UK to get back to her. Any specific request I made of her was delivered on time though. The jury was still out on that one.

Sean was making great headway with recruiting the staff. He was conducting all the staff interviews with the relevant depot manager, of which we now had all nine, as well as the Le Bourget manager.

With nothing to show the applicants in most cases, it was back to telling the story of a business which is rewarding for everybody involved, and where you are defined not by your education or qualifications, but by your energy, commitment and enthusiasm.

I had noticed when interviewing with Didier that he made a big deal of each applicant's education, be it the qualifications they attained or indeed the institution in which they studied. Didier's explanation for this was that it gives applicants an area of conversation where they are relaxed, and therefore he gets a better idea of them as individuals. Whilst I can see that as a justification for that strategy, I couldn't help but notice that people without stories of academic greatness were never interviewed in the first place.

For the depot interviews, Sean had adopted a light touch interview policy of giving as many people as possible a chance to tell their own story in their own words, rather than a regimented 'French' interview that could easily take two hours each. This also gave each depot manager the greatest number of people to choose from for their staff. Sean and I had done this on many occasions in the past and had a good sense of the sort of person that we needed, so once Sean had identified the people he thought we needed, it was just a matter of convincing the manager. This was the tricky bit; if you tell someone to do something, they will do it, but you still have the ownership on your shoulders should it go wrong. However, if you can gently nudge the manager in the direction you require, without making it too obvious, then you get exactly the people you want, and with someone else going home at night worrying if they've made the right choice. Phrases like '...it's completely up to you, but if it were my decision...' and '...It's your business, but if you want my opinion...' are very useful expressions in this regard.

35

While Sean was coercing his victims into recruitment submission, I was working on the plan for the trip to the UK. The later we could leave it, the more people we would have to take with us, but a later visit would start to eat into the time we needed for training and stock deliveries, so it was a balancing act.

After speaking to my UK colleagues and suppliers about their own availability to conduct tours and presentations of their own parts of the business, I concluded that the 9th to the 12th of August was the best time and it would give us about 40 people to take for a trip covering three nights in the north of England. Armed with this information, I could crack on with the arrangements.

36

As Sean was in Paris conducting interviews, and I wanted to be in that area the next day to meet Madame Dupont, I went down to have dinner with him to get a recruitment update. The Imperial was full, so we were in a place called Hotel California just off the Champs-Élysées. I must admit, I booked it based on the name alone.

Built in the 1920s, the Hotel California used to be a large private home, and the rooms and public areas still maintained a homely feel to them. There were paintings dotted about the place that looked valuable to me, but then again, I know nothing of such matters. Also, in the public areas, there were various sculptures, vases and other artistic exhibits that were inside glass cases. It had a nice vibe to it.

When I checked in at the front desk, the young man waiting was wearing a black waistcoat with gold buttons on it, a white shirt and a gold bow tie. He looked like he was a descendent of the original staff of the family home in 1924. I put my bag down and said hello, to which he replied with a wide smile, 'Welcome to the Hotel California.' That was it, the song was in my head now and it didn't matter what I did, I could not shake it off. For a while at least…

I went to the room that I had reserved; it was only a basic room at a reasonable rate. Once inside the room, I sorted my case out and opened the door that I assumed led into the bathroom. What I entered was a large sitting room with a dining table in it and a flight of stairs leading up to two more bedrooms and two bathrooms. This was a heck of an upgrade, but I assumed that it was something they did for first timers now and again to make an impression. It had certainly done that.

Surveying my new estate, I decided on the larger of the two bedrooms in my newly named 'East Wing' as it had the better equipped bathroom. I had a quick shower and then went downstairs and watched some TV while I was waiting for beer o'clock to arrive.

A half hour into a fascinating programme about the day's political shenanigans in France, I heard a click. I turned to where I thought I had heard it from and was being stared at by a family of four with an abundance of luggage and a black cocker spaniel. After the mutual cry of 'What are you doing in my room?' we called reception and a manager came up to get these interlopers out of my room.

When the lady arrived to sort out the confusion, it quickly transpired that my room was the original one I had entered, and the door that I thought was to the bathroom should have been locked. I had ended up in the family suite next door. I sheepishly gathered my belongings and made the retreat into my much more modest accommodation.

I left the room with two thoughts. Firstly, it could have been a lot more embarrassing than it actually was and, secondly, I hoped they didn't intend using that toilet.

37

It was during July that some of the more problematic aspects of employment law and bonus payments were coming to the surface. We had recruited the initial few staff on a standard off-the-shelf contract that Didier had used in the past. This gave us the time to get our own house in order before they got their real contracts. Didier had been working closely with Madame Dupont on the outstanding points and they now needed finalising, so I went back to her offices in the 8th.

The principle of giving managers a percentage of the profits each month is supposed to be a motivational tool. It certainly had been in the UK and USA. The only proviso with this scheme was that the manager had to prove he could protect the company's assets and integrity. To this end, to be included in the profit-related bonus scheme, the manager had to agree to pay for any financial losses to the depot that the manager could reasonably have avoided, out of their bonuses. Whilst this might sound a little draconian, the alternative is to pay the manager the same, much less rewarding, bonus scheme as the staff. When faced with this choice, every manager that I had ever witnessed had agreed to the deal. This meant that the arrangement needed to be formalised and in the contract, and this is where it got problematic.

The French government is very happy for companies to pay staff bonuses. It is, however, much less keen on companies charging staff in a scheme like ours. As Madame Dupont pointed out, 'The default position for French people is that companies are not to be trusted, and that the government is there to protect them from greedy management.' My pleading that our intention was to pay people a lot of money, but only on a fair basis, was met by deaf ears and a Gallic shrug.

Allied to this was the fact that bonuses, if paid monthly, could be viewed as an integral part of an individual's salary after a period of time and could not be taken away without agreement from the staff member. An agreement that I assumed was somewhat difficult to secure.

I reiterated to Madame Dupont that all I wanted to do was give money to our staff, but on a fair and reasonable basis. Her reply was, 'Mr Simpson, your definition of fair and reasonable, and the government's definition, are probably quite different.'

Once again, and after several hours of my blood pressure reaching dangerously high levels, we managed to find a way through these issues with different terminology and caveats. We couldn't call any monies withheld from staff a 'retention' or 'charge', but we could call it a *'contribution'*. It all seemed meaningless to me, but so long as Madame Dupont signed it off, we could all totter off headlong into the next set of lengthy debates. I made a mental note to myself to get my blood pressure pills upgraded. I hoped that there were some super-strong pills that doctors kept locked away in a safe, only to be unleashed when they heard the word 'France'.

38

That night, Sean and I were back in the Imperial, and therefore, McGuires ahead of, what was so far, France's finest food – the Indian restaurant just down the road.

Sean's day had been good, in that he managed to find four or five people that looked like they might be good. I was encouraged by this and said to Sean that the main thing here is that the manager is currently at home telling his or her partner that *they* had found some good people. The point being about ownership, or at least *perceived* ownership. There was no way we were going to get every recruitment choice correct between us on Day One, but at least if the manager felt that it was their choice to recruit each person, they would try much harder to make the business work with those people. If the manager reached the point where they couldn't work with someone, I wanted it to be the manager that felt that they had made a mistake, not Sean. There is a subtle art to getting exactly what you want, with other people believing that it was their choice all along, and it was something I had worked hard to achieve over the years. Having satisfied myself that Sean was doing all he could to maintain this ethos, we downed a couple of swift cold ones, and wandered off to get our curry.

Suri's had become our culinary sanctuary. It was as if the French food couldn't harm us all the time we knew we had Suri's to head back to sometime soon.

Owned and run by Mr and Mrs Patel, it had a very authentic feel to it. One or both of them were usually front of house, and Suri herself would always be adorned in beautifully traditional Indian dress. She was the artist in the relationship, and her husband, Rohan, was very much the businessman. They had gone out of their way to make us feel welcome from the very first time we walked through their door, and over the months that we had been using them, we had started sharing the story of the business we were creating. Rohan was intrigued about how we were going to change the purchasing habits of a nation in terms of how they buy kitchens, whereas Suri, on the other hand, couldn't wait for us to open as she wanted a new kitchen herself.

During our reassuringly good dinner that night, I asked Sean if he thought that our new managers might like to come here. It is an integral part of Eastney Interiors' philosophy to take the teams out regularly. It's a good thing to do on its own merit, but also, you get to hear more about what is really going on in the business, and what their issues are, when they've had a glass of wine.

In the UK business, Indian restaurants were used most of the time for team dinners. This being because you can phone an order through in advance and just have many dishes of different curries on the table for the team to choose from. This removes the possibility of someone's order being messed up or forgotten altogether so that the conversation during the evening can be about the business and the people, rather than the food. I was only too aware of the role that restaurant food played in French society, but I was keen to try it anyway. We could put the managers up in the Imperial and make a bit of an event out of it. Sean didn't care about any of that, he was just grateful that he could pencil in another night of curry.

39

Back in Lille the next day, I had arranged to meet Claude, Yasmine, our IT manager, and Camille Boucher, our property manager, at the Lille depot in Seclin, where we were going to have our head office. The quicker we could get the office ready, the quicker we could stop spending money on meeting rooms in hotels and get the support guys and girls into a normal work routine as well as getting a team spirit established.

Upon arrival I was met, as usual, by a group of fitters standing outside smoking. I was starting to find this slightly reassuring in a bizarre sort of way. Maybe it was a sign that everything was under control and that no panic was needed. I chose to believe that, anyway.

Yasmine, Claude and Camille were already inside the building when I walked in. A cursory glance around told me that the walls were up and painted, we had a ceiling of sorts with cables hanging out everywhere and the floor looked like it had been prepared and was waiting for some sort of covering. Some small offices had been built; inside one was a plastic table and a few chairs, and it was in this room that I found the team. It turned out that this room was the kitchen and the fitters had made it their base. While the rest of the offices were in a state of disarray, the area dedicated to the coffee machine most definitely wasn't.

I asked Camille for an update and, more importantly, when we could move in. She said, 'Well, it depends what you mean by *move in*.' When we had established that I meant everybody being able to come here every day and function normally, she replied, 'Middle of September.' I was just about start a lecture about what 'quick' actually meant, when Yasmine piped up, 'Yes, sorry Peter, that's my fault.'

We could get the building completed internally in about two weeks' time, taking us to the end of July. We could also get all the support equipment like printers installed. We could even get the server installed, which was a mammoth task, but was being done by the UK guys. What we couldn't get before the middle of September was the phone lines and Wi-Fi installed. This was being provided by one of the national providers, who, just like my previous experiences, move with the speed and agility of a wounded sloth. The real issue, however, was that Yasmine hadn't placed the order when she needed to, and we would now be delayed by about six weeks because of it.

This was not good. I just stood there trying to digest this latest setback without saying anything and it was Claude that finally piped up that there was a way around this, but that it was going to be expensive.

He and Yasmine drifted into jargon mode for a few minutes, which was the first time I had heard Yasmine do this and was one small positive to come from this calamity. Claude then said, 'To cut a long story short we can get what are, effectively, industrial sized SIM cards that can cope with the amount of data and the speed of connectivity that we need to function normally here, but it will probably cost us about 50,000 euros for the period that we need them.'

That was 50,000 euros on top of the 50,000 euros that I was going to spend on the UK trip that wasn't in Fiona's numbers. Far from opening a ten-depot test in France, at this rate I would be lucky to open a market stall near the Louvre.

40

Claude was proving himself to be an excellent recruit, even if you could never get a word in edgeways when around him. I spoke to Sean about an idea I had been considering around making Claude the 'Head of Depot Support', which would mean that the other department heads would report directly to him instead of me. This had a few benefits in that if there were any dismissals, aside from Sean and Claude, they wouldn't be my responsibility and therefore I could legitimately hear any appeals that came from those decisions. From a leadership perspective, it also made the decision-making process much more agile, with fewer people to include. Finally, on the finance side, it made sense to me to have an accountant scrutinising expenses across all the departments on a regular basis. On the downside, it distanced me slightly from the support team, but with the size of the business and the amount of social time we spent together, this would be manageable. It would mean that Sean and Claude were on an equal footing and would be working much closer together. Sean was fine with this, and so I invited Claude out with Sean and myself in Lille to run it past him.

I decided to go to an up-market French restaurant for this dinner as it would hopefully be a happy event that we could all have good memories about. After a small amount of research, a restaurant called La Mer was chosen in the old town. This was an establishment famous for its oysters; indeed, the front part of the building was a fish shop that you walked through to get to the restaurant at the back.

Once in the restaurant part, the opulence was staggering. A very high ceiling and tables spread sparsely across the room gave the feel of a banqueting hall from an 18th-century mansion. Vast chandeliers hanging at four points in the room gave just enough light to feel very private at your table. In the corner was a pianist wearing a tuxedo and bow tie quietly playing French classics. There were clues everywhere that this was not going to be a cheap evening.

The maître d' led us through to our table, checking our dress code casually as we walked through. I'm not sure that he fully approved of our smart jeans and shirts, but he didn't say anything – if you exclude what he said with his eyes that is.

We played the dining game in this high-class restaurant with the usual theatre around the menu and the wine, and he disappeared, to return some minutes later with a bottle of white wine and a bottle of red.

Once the wine was poured, he took both bottles to a smaller table about two metres away from us. When I asked why the wine wasn't on our table, he just said that he would make sure that we had enough wine.

We had a good time that night. Claude was over the moon that he had been promoted already and he couldn't wait to tell his wife, Fleur. We made plans about how we were going to run the business and we laughed a lot. During our conversation, our wine ran dry, and with no-one noticing that we were bereft, Sean got up from his chair and picked up the wine bottles. From out of nowhere, the maître d' appeared and tried to snatch the wine from Sean's hand. Sean, unperturbed by this, held onto his bounty diligently. A polite yet comical tug of war ensued over the bottles until the red wine fell to the floor and smashed. The maître d' was clearly unhappy with this, muttering under his breath that we were ignorant heathens that didn't deserve to be in his restaurant. Claude and I contributed to the event unfolding before us by staring straight down and trying not to laugh.

The evening definitely provided the memories I was hoping for, but maybe not in exactly the way I imagined.

41

The Arc de Triomphe had long been a mystery to me. As far as I could make out, there were just two rules. Firstly, you should broadly drive anticlockwise around it, and secondly, you should broadly give way to traffic entering the system.

I say 'broadly' because at any given time you will see faint glimpses of the rules being observed, but these brief occurrences are most likely to be first timers, who haven't yet mastered the gladiatorial nature of this magnificent beast.

It is about five lanes wide all the way around, but if there were ever any lane markings, they have long since disappeared, and there are 12 roads that enter it. The number of entry points leading to the name the French give it – *L'étoile*, or *The Star*.

The chaos of this roundabout is exacerbated by the fact that each of the 12 roads that join it do have street names on the lampposts nearby, but the signs are about 200mm by 100mm and, therefore, if you don't actually know where you need to exit, you have to swing across to the right to be able to read the tiny sign, then swing back to the middle when you realise that it wasn't your exit. Alternatively, you could just crawl around in the outside lane and get bombarded by Exocet-like traffic merging into the melee.

However, for all its eccentricities, the Arc de Triomphe works, and it works well. I firmly believe that if you tried to strictly regulate it, as would most certainly be the case in the UK, the whole of Paris would come to a grinding halt.

More than that, I think that this incredible road intersection is a metaphor for the whole of France, in that there are definitely rules, but everybody just uses them as a guideline and, actually, it works better that way.

But it was early August now, and the large conurbations in the north of France were virtually empty. It was so quiet that my dealings with the Arc de Triomphe were pleasant affairs that took mere seconds.

It wasn't just the Arc that was empty though. Just about every bar, restaurant and shop was closed as the owners and staff of these establishments disappeared to the south of France for their holidays. It is such a huge exodus that I often wondered if there were some tectonic consequence of this annual shift.

What it meant to us was that organising the logistics on the French side for our trip to the UK had been severely hampered by everything and everybody that we wanted to utilise being unavailable. We had to put the staff from Paris in hotels near Lille the night before departure, and even trying to get a meal organised for them was very difficult. The larger hotels remained open during August, but with limited facilities, so you would be very lucky if the bar or restaurant were open, even in the multi-national hotel chains. In the end, we had to say to everyone to just sort themselves out for food, as it proved impossible to book a table for the 20-odd people that we had to cater for.

42

We left within 30 minutes of our planned departure time the next morning. I had remembered what Madame Dupont had told me about punctuality and had instructed everyone to be at the meeting point one full hour before we needed to leave, so we were actually a half hour ahead of time. One to me.

We were only 32 people by the time August 9th had arrived, as a few people had decided not to join us, and a few others still managed to sneak away on holiday. This was fine as I was already beginning to regret my impetuous suggestion of a trip to the UK due to the problems of getting fed last night and then again getting everyone onto the coach this morning. It had been like 'Whac-A-Mole' where I managed to extricate people away from their cigarettes and onto the coach, and then 30 seconds later when I looked out again, someone else had escaped for a crafty puff.

We were booked onto the Eurotunnel, which reduced the opportunities to lose people in transit compared to a ferry. Thirty-five minutes later, we emerged in the Queen's country at Folkestone and I gave a symbolic wave out of the train window to my long-suffering wife, whom I barely saw at the moment, save for a few hours at weekends and occasionally when I needed to be in London for meetings, and could sneak in a crafty night at home at the same time.

43

We headed to York, where I had arranged a pub dinner of fish and chips for the first night. The pub we were in, The Old Black Horse, had a private room at the back so that we could spread out a bit and make some noise. This was the first time that I had met a lot of the depot staff, so I had decided to say a few words of welcome at the start of the dinner.

At the pre-dinner drinks in the hotel, it was already clear that people were sticking to their own groups. This was not unusual or unexpected, but in this group of people there were distinctly different types, all sticking to themselves.

Sean and I had agreed to take on the first batch of managers based on gut feel rather than experience or academic excellence, and this had resulted in a very cosmopolitan tranche of people. These managers had recruited their own teams and, unsurprisingly, we ended up with teams in the same mould as the managers.

Sean pointed out Ahmet from Turkey who was his first recruit. Ahmet had recommended Eastney Interiors to a couple of his friends and we had ended up with three managers from Turkey, who in turn recruited several more Turks in their teams. By looking at the drinks in front of these people, it appeared that most of them were not strict Muslims.

In a different area was Carlos, a second generation Portuguese national who was laughing with four other people, whom I assumed he had recruited.

Stood at the bar was the office team. Claude was in the middle of telling a story, the wise money on it being about Booboo.

Then, in a very separate area, were about 12 people that were sitting noticeably quieter than the other groups. Sean said that these were the French depot teams, some from Paris but mainly from the north.

When we had herded them onto the coach and arrived at the

restaurant, I said a few words of welcome and told them that we were here to understand a bit more about our corporate culture and objectives, but just as important was to have fun and get to know each other in environments like this. A polite round of applause followed my address, and the feast commenced.

Surveying the plates of fish and chips at the end of the meal, they fell into three categories. Firstly, were the people that just ate and enjoyed it. This was, regrettably, the minority. Secondly, was the group that ate the bare minimum and then tried to squeeze the leftovers into one side of their plate with their cutlery to make it look like they had eaten half of their dinner. Thirdly, were the people that managed to eat the fish but without eating any of the batter. These plates looked like they harboured cod-like exoskeletons.

Desert was jam roly-poly with custard, and the spilt was only two ways on this one. About 20 per cent of the plates went back to the kitchen clear of this heavenly delight, with the other 80 per cent going back completely untouched.

With wine freely available on the tables and then whisky, brandy and port put down for good measure, people were loosening up nicely, but still staying very noticeably in their own social groups, so I had to make a bit of an effort to mix things up a bit. I started with the department managers, telling them to float around and chat. Didier was already doing this almost instinctively, but I had to nudge the others out of their comfort zone. I don't believe in forced enjoyment, a mantra which means I rarely go out on New Years' Eve, so I left it at that for now and, after an hour or so, bundled everyone back on the coach to go back to the hotel. I retired immediately, and asked Sean and Claude to stay up to make sure that no harm came to anyone.

44

The next morning was a quiet affair. The immediate issue being to get everyone out of their beds and onto the coach again to visit some UK depots.

Sean looked like death warmed up, and when I asked him what time he had gone to bed, he said he had no idea, but it wasn't long ago. I managed to finally get Claude to answer his phone and he too eventually surfaced, looking like an extra from *Silent Witness*.

Once I had got these two up, it was up to them to get the rest of their teams ready to leave, so I could then sit back and enjoy my newspaper, coffee and juice in peace.

Departure time was 8am, and at 7.30am I started checking that we had accounted for everybody. At that point, we were still missing five people, all from the depot teams and Sean assured me that the managers of those depots were on the case. I asked him to put a bit of weight behind it, and he got up to do this, but looked like he might deposit last night's meal on the carpet at any time.

8am came and went, and we were still missing two people. We had no choice but to ask the hotel staff to go into the rooms, as our knocking and phoning had failed to get a response. Reluctantly, they did this, and the first of them was found fast asleep in bed wearing headphones with music still blaring away. The other was discovered in his bathroom, awake but not in best form, with his head down the toilet.

We decided to leave the wounded soldier in barracks for the day and set off with the others to see the UK business.

Given the poorly state of several of the entourage, the day went well. I had primed each UK depot manager that we were visiting to talk about the ownership element of the business and about how the profit-related bonus meant that their lifestyle was in their own hands, being mindful that it was a mixed audience. The French team asked questions along the way, and in each depot our guys were taking copious amounts of photographs.

In the coach between depots, I was asking the team how they felt about the positive stories they had been hearing, and all of them said that they were impressed, but when I tried to push them about what their own depot story might look like, they were slightly evasive, highlighting points about team morale and togetherness, rather than profits and bonuses.

45

Dinner was a calmer affair on the second night. I had booked a hotel in Sheffield as we were visiting our kitchen supplier in Rotherham the next day. This hotel had a large function room and had agreed to do a traditional Sunday roast beef for us even though it was only Wednesday.

There was definitely more integration on the second night of the trip. People were gathered in one big group at the bar before dinner rather than several smaller ones. There was much mocking of our wounded soldier, who it must be said, still didn't look too good and was holding a glass of iced water. Stories were told of last night's fish and chip supper and the high jinks at the bar afterwards. It was starting to feel like the business that I wanted it to be. During the chat, it transpired that Sean was the final one to go to bed the previous evening, and the best guess at a time by piecing together other people's stories was that it was at 6am.

The roast dinner was better received than the fish and chips, although my French friends didn't quite know what to make of the Yorkshire puddings. My toast that evening included the comment that they could now all claim to be honorary 'rosbifs', which raised a titter. People still sat in their own groups, but there were distinctly more inter-group exchanges that night.

Even though the hotel bar was again available for late night *digestifs*, I noticed that most of the Turks and Portuguese went to bed fairly early and that it was the French that stayed up later. Sean said that the French contingent had been by far the more sensible and reserved the previous night, which enabled them to still enjoy a late-night drink the following evening. Very wise.

46

We managed to leave on time and in full to get to the kitchen supplier on the Thursday. Talk about small victories; this seemed like a major milestone. I still had the 'Whac-a-mole' cigarette game to play before the bus could leave, but it was a victory, nonetheless.

The supplier had a vast manufacturing unit in Rotherham and there was a significant amount of health and safety to comply with. This started before we even got off the coach, with the gatekeeper coming aboard and giving us several dos and don'ts. We were told exactly where to park, and then there were several hi-vis clad people waiting at the coach door to escort us into the building. They had eyes on us all the time, almost waiting for someone to break rank so they could leap on them. These people looked like they could get a job with the French government checking invoices and staff rotas.

When safely confined in a meeting room, there was more housekeeping to deal with. This included a video of the history of the company, sheets to fill in and sign, some maps showing the layout of the building and, most importantly for my team, where the smoking shelter was. It wasn't anywhere nearby, that was for sure.

After the talk, and with all the sheets signed and collected, we were asked to wait while our escorts arrived to collect us. A few of the team said that they were going for a quick puff, followed by a few more and a few more until there were only about seven of us left in the room.

It took no longer than five minutes. I heard very gruff and upset voices coming from downstairs somewhere. Within seconds, my team were being frogmarched back into the room and one of the hi-vis heavies asked who the team leader was. When I put my hand up, he came to me and said, rather sternly, 'Could you *please* keep control of where your people smoke.'

It turned out that rather than walk the hundred metres to the designated smoking area, our delegation had gone straight outside the front door of the meeting building and collectively lit up. This had been picked up by CCTV and security from the front gate had been immediately dispatched in a minibus to the scene of the crime. I apologised, but when I spoke to the team about it afterwards, they genuinely couldn't see what they had done wrong. Why did they need to go to a smoking shelter when it wasn't raining?

47

We spent our last night in the UK back in York. Sean's local knowledge and contacts meant that we could show our entourage a proper night out in a few pubs, followed by a Chinese dinner. I would have preferred curry myself, but Sean insisted that his local Chinese was good. It was certainly preferable to a curry for our entourage.

The area around the Shambles in York is a tremendous night out, and the team loved all the really old pubs that just ooze character and stories. With no attempt on my part to get people of mixed backgrounds mingling together, they all socialised together as one. The layout of many of the old pubs in York is not conducive to sitting down, so people naturally moved around more and conversed. I noticed that Claude was sat down with Yasmine in one of the pubs we visited, and she looked a little upset. Best keep out of it, I decided.

The Chinese meal was enjoyed by everyone. I had ordered many different dishes to be put in the middle of the table for everyone to help themselves, and it went down well. Sean was right, it was very good food.

During the meal I was seated next to Claude and when the opportunity arose to speak privately, I asked him what the story was with Yasmine. He told me that she was considering leaving. This wasn't because she didn't like the job or the company, far from it, she had thoroughly enjoyed her time so far and that was what was making her so upset. Her issue was that she was used to having a larger team of people around her, and being now in a team of just two, her and one assistant, was exposing her weaknesses to the point where she didn't think she could do the job justice.

When I asked Claude for his opinion on the matter, he said that he thought she was a very good person but needed more support than we anticipated. When I asked if he thought he could provide that support, he said that with greater help from the UK, he did. I knew the right people in the UK to assist with this issue so we decided, over a spare rib, that we would continue working with her to help her reach her potential with us. Not a very French way to decide on an issue, but hey ho, we were in York!

The last night went without incident back at the hotel bar, with the first night antics now a dim and distant memory. People were just sitting or standing together laughing. The trip had been a success. I was now looking at one team of people who all had a common goal, but with different roles to play. The stories that would come from this visit would last forever, and the people that weren't able to come for whatever reason, would want a trip to the UK of their own. Mission accomplished.

48

Back in the depressing reality of France in mid-August, with nothing happening anywhere, and no-one to shout at about it, I had some time with Sean and Claude to see where we were in all areas, and particularly regarding systems.

It wasn't looking too bad overall, but it needed a lot of things to happen in the final two weeks before we opened, largely around getting stock into the depots, and getting everyone trained on the systems. Sean and Yasmine were going to deliver the systems training, and I was going to help Henri co-ordinate the stock deliveries. Claude, for his part, was filling gaps that had been left in various departments. Straight after this meeting, he was off to Paris to meet up with an insurance agent. He said that he had been getting more requests from Fiona for detail on committed funds lately, and he wasn't sure why.

I was about to find out…

49

Bernard had been getting quite tetchy at our recent bi-weekly executive meetings in London, with noticeably more obtuse questions of Fiona regarding costs. At times like these, I always adopted the same plan – say as little as possible, and don't speak unless spoken to. There was no avoiding it during a meeting in London on Tuesday 30th August though.

To start the meeting, Fiona went through all the business divisions' finances, these being the core business of Bullings, and the three different Eastney Interiors' businesses in the UK, Florida and France.

Bullings sales were by far the highest of the divisions, but profitability was declining, and the length and cost of the retail property leases was making the overall picture increasingly complicated.

The UK arm of Eastney was performing well, with sales still growing and profitability high. The business in Florida had lost its way a bit in recent times, with some deep-rooted cultural issues in the southern states creating friction between the troops that affected profitability. There was still a trajectory of sales growth in the USA though.

And then there was France. The page of the presentation that described my business was just a sea of red ink. No income, just costs and commitments. It wasn't pretty.

At the end of the presentation, Bernard said, 'What this business needs is strong leaders, people who can make a difference to things, people who can make bad things better.'

He asked the four of us that controlled the sales subsidiaries to do a five-year profitability plan, and also an exit plan. After some more detail from Fiona, we were allowed a coffee break. As I got up to leave the room, Bernard said, 'Peter, can I have a minute?'

When we were alone, he said, 'Now then Peter, I want you to think long and hard about your business. There is no shame in saying that we think it's going to be too much hard work compared to the UK and pull the plug today. There is great shame, however, in continuing to plough this particular furrow to just decide that it doesn't work in 12 months' time.'

I said, 'I understand that Bernard, but I haven't even started trading yet, please be reasonable.'

To which he smiled and replied, 'Peter, you know I'm not here to be reasonable.'

Over a coffee in the room next to the boardroom, I said to Fiona, 'Jeez, where did that little lot come from?'

She said, 'It's been on the cards for a while now, he's been getting grief from upstairs.' When I asked her to elaborate, she quickly scanned the room to see who was around, and said in almost a whisper, 'The success of the trade business in the UK has prompted the board to challenge him on the company's overall focus, especially as the Bullings business is such a big beast, but you didn't hear that from me, understood?'

'Understood.'

50

Heading back to Lille on the Eurostar, I called Sean and Claude and asked them to meet me at the Crest that night. I then used the rest of the time on the train to think about the story I needed.

It wasn't just tonight that I needed a story for; I needed one for the wider team on an ongoing basis. I especially needed one for Bernard and, ideally, it would be the same story to all. I had sold the business so far based on a dream, but I needed more than that now. A dream is fine but for something to be tangible, it needed foundations, something firm that we could build on. And therein lay the problem, we had no history to build on, no customers or market to point to, no competitors to cite, we had nothing except ourselves.

Hmm, except ourselves...

At the Crest that night, I ran through the day's events and detailed the two plans that we had to create for about two weeks' time. Sean was shocked, but Claude was mortified. He had left perfectly good employment to come to Eastney Intérieurs, and five minutes after doing an investment plan, he was having to do an exit plan.

Rather than wallow in corporate self-pity, I said, 'Look guys, we have created a company from nothing, just a pipedream from these two strange English guys that arrived a few months ago. Now we've got about 40 people, several depots, an office we can almost use, stock rolling into the distribution centre in the next week or so, and an opening date in about four weeks' time. That is already more than many people achieve in a lifetime. However, we actually have more than that, much more, and we saw it during the trip to the UK. We have energy.'

I paused for a moment to take stock of my audience and to have a swig of coffee after my majestic speech. Sean was staring out of the window at the traffic, and Claude looked up from his laptop and said, 'That's all very well Pete, but where do I put that on my spreadsheet?'

Somewhat deflated, I said, 'Claude, give Fiona whatever she asks for regarding the numbers, but the numbers won't save us, they are ugly. We can increase sales forecasts as high as we want, but why should anyone believe them? No, the story is in the people, and that is what we are going to submit to the board. Our people, *our story*.'

51

It was Claude's first curry that night, and I was surprised at how much he enjoyed it. He picked from the selection I had ordered and asked if they did anything spicier. This was very unusual for a French national, but they gave him an extra spicy vindaloo which he said he enjoyed. I had a taste, and while it was pleasant, in terms of spice it was only as hot as a British Madras at most.

Our ramblings that evening were about the best ever cover version song. I instigated this line of discussion as I already believed I knew the winner; it was *Live and Let Die* by Guns N' Roses. Sean had a different view, he thought it was *Feeling Good* by Muse. That was a tremendous shout and made me think twice about my choice. Claude sat quietly, face down in his vindaloo, while we were arguing the toss about the two songs. Eventually, he piped up with, 'You're both wrong, it's *My Way* by Frank Sinatra.' Sean and I stopped talking and stared at him. When I asked him to justify this outrageous claim, he said, 'He just ripped off *Comme d'habitude* by Claude François but made it one of the best-known songs on the planet. I think you'll find that meets your criteria for the purposes of this discussion.'

As the self-appointed adjudicator in these most important matters, I gave it to Claude that night. Partly for his bare-faced cheek, and partly because he'd already been through quite enough for one day.

We re-grouped in the morning to form our plan for the next few days. Foremost in my mind was getting the numbers and presentation done to get the lion off my back. I was going to start the presentation with the numbers, but in a very matter of fact way. I wasn't going to change any of the forecasts, I was just going to add exit costs by year at the foot of each column. This would all be on one page of, mainly, red ink.

After that, I was going to highlight some of the individuals that had joined us and describe their story. I would use photos and videos to show the energy that I wanted to convey and give the story life. There were no time limits for the presentation set by Fiona, but in my mind the whole thing needed to take a maximum of 15 minutes.

We also had the small matter of a trade kitchen business to open, so Sean and Claude were going to keep everyone and everything on track while I was out in the depots and office, filming random events and people – well, that was what it would look like anyway. There was nothing to be gained by telling anyone else about the situation we were in, so we decided to keep it to ourselves.

I bought a decent video camera and stand and gave myself a crash course in how to use it. I was going to get film of people telling their story in a casual environment, and then film action in the depots and office of everyday life happening and a business being created by those people. I was going to need some help later turning these random chunks of film into a polished 15-minute presentation but, one step at a time. There was no point in filming either Sean or myself as everyone knew us, so I started with Claude.

52

Due to Claude knowing the full story, he was more verbose than normal in his talk about himself, I suspect through desperation of not wanting the business to close. We had to stop several times while he was talking, simply because he didn't seem to pause for breath and that fact was going to make the video difficult to edit later. We got there in the end though, and I thought he came across well. I did the same with Didier and Henri at the office, and then moved on to the depots.

I filmed a few managers setting up their depots with their teams and it was useful to see how the depots were progressing, but I was missing the energy I was looking for; the energy that I had witnessed in the UK. Ahmet and his colleagues from Turkey were quite effusive on camera, but the French guys were being very reserved.

It was time to kill two birds with one stone. I had said to Sean that I wanted to take the team to Suri's for a curry in Paris, and I also wanted to capture the energy that I knew they had inside them but kept locked up most of the time. I hoped that over a curry I would see the side of them that told our story the best.

We hastily arranged the rooms, the restaurant and the team for the following Monday, 5th September. We could muster eight of the nine managers, three department heads, Sean, Claude and myself.

We had a couple of drinks in the Imperial Hotel to start with, and I was filming randomly as they chatted. Once they had noticed me each time though, there was almost no point in carrying on as they clammed up, so I had to be quite discrete.

At the restaurant, they were laughing nervously as the food arrived. Most of the French contingent had never had curry and were looking at the plates before them with more than a little trepidation. The Turks were more relaxed about it, particularly as I was able to say that all the meat was halal in this particular establishment.

The portions of food that some of them took for themselves were pitiful. The merest scraping off the top of the plate of deliciousness in front of them with a half spoon of rice. I had to help here, and I did so by dolloping huge swathes of different food on their plates so they could just dig in and see what they liked. It must be said that the few extra bottles of red wine I had placed around the table were helping me start to see the energy that I wanted to capture.

I was filming both from my seat and from a distance, and I thought it was going quite well. At the end of the meal, I was standing in the bar area, paying the bill, when Claude decided to start a rendition of *Comme d'habitude*. I hadn't asked for this, and I suspect it was the wine that inspired him more than the omnipresent camera but that didn't matter. The team all joined in with Claude and then cheered themselves at the end. It looked good.

The state of the plates at the end of the meal was somewhat predictable. The Turks had cleared their plates, and the French plates still contained almost everything I had previously dumped on them, largely untouched. There was one French manager that enjoyed it, and I remember saying to Sean, 'That guy will go far.'

53

The next day, I had over two hours of film when I arrived at the production company at La Défense, not far from the hotel. I met with Monsieur Lavigne, who looked to me like he should have been in the queue for his school milk. However, after listening patiently to the story of his business for 30 minutes or so, we finally got down to talking about my requirements. He listened well and made some suggestions, most of which were a bit too elaborate for what I had in mind. I wanted it to show the energy of the team and the creation of a business in just 15 minutes, rather than an abundance of clever production. He said he would need two days to do this. With this arranged, I went to Le Bourget to see the new distribution centre and the stock that was currently arriving.

Hugo Fournier had joined us to be a depot manager originally, but when the plan to bring the distribution centre in-house was revealed, he applied to be the manager. He had completed five years in the military when he was younger, and he said to us that his experience there, which was mainly in the stores, would help him keep an orderly ship at Le Bourget.

On arrival, I was met with a car park full of lorries and a very stressed-out Hugo running around between them. I went inside and started chatting to the warehouse staff we had recruited, who were calmly sitting in the staff kitchen drinking coffee. They told me that without any systems yet, the pallets needed to be unloaded in a specific way to make the products easier to locate later on when they needed to load the trucks for the depots. When the systems were up and running, they would know exactly where each pallet was going before they had even unloaded it, but for now, it was mayhem.

I called Claude and Yasmine and managed to ascertain that the systems were still a week away, and that was before any training. It was going to be the best part of two weeks before the distribution centre could function normally, and probably another week while they tidied up the stock so that it could be picked properly for delivery. That left less than two weeks to get everything out to the depots and ready to sell.

Hugo finally calmed down a bit about a half an hour after I arrived, and I was having a coffee with him in his office. Here was a man that clearly took pride in the job, but by the fact that he was just about coming down from the ceiling with stress and his staff were nonchalantly plodding around the warehouse looking at pallets of ovens, I deduced that he wasn't that keen on delegation.

When I raised this point, he said, 'It's not that I can't delegate, you have to understand that these people are here on a fairly low wage, and they don't expect to have to challenge themselves too much during their 35 hours to justify that pay.'

This was a disappointment. Two of the junior staff here were on the trip to the UK, and I had assumed that the energy and relationships that I had witnessed developing on that trip would transfer directly into their commitment in the workplace. It would appear that, in this instance at least, that wasn't the case.

I asked Hugo if he thought that increasing their pay would increase their commitment, and he said, 'It's quite unlikely; I will assess each of them over the next few months and then make one of them my assistant manager. The title is more likely to increase commitment than any increase in pay today.'

Well, at least he had a plan; I just hoped that he didn't have a heart attack while he executed it.

In McGuires that night, I was telling Sean about my day, and specifically about the issue with commitment at Le Bourget. He said that he was seeing a similar tale in the depots, but that it wasn't everyone. There was a vast majority of people that saw no connection between the fun and laughter in York, and their day-to-day life at work. He said that there was a noticeable difference between the humour and energy in the depots run by the Turks and Portuguese compared to the French nationals. I was struggling with this; they were all French citizens, just of different backgrounds. Why should they be so different?

54

Back at La Défense a couple of days later, I was waiting eagerly to meet Monsieur Lavigne to review the video, post-production. It was now Thursday, and I had to present this in London on the following Monday.

Even though I had already sat through the history of his company for half an hour on Tuesday, I wasn't excused from a tour of the production area where they worked their magic today. I must admit, it was impressive, although it looked a bit like a recording studio to me, with an area behind glass with a microphone in the middle of the room, and lots of faders and screens this side of the glass. I had the equipment explained to me before I was eventually allowed to sit down and watch my video.

What I had asked for was a punchy, 15-minute video showing energy, commitment and a group of people that were worthy of investment. What I got was a 25-minute video showing the managers talking about their teams in a very philosophical and ethereal way. He hadn't even included the clip of them singing *Comme d'habitude* for Heaven's sake.

At the end, I just stared at him. I didn't know quite what to say really. He started explaining his reasoning, saying that he had 'painted a picture with words' regarding the energy of the group. Well, it wasn't any energy form that I recognized, and if I showed that to Bernard, it wouldn't get past the five-minute mark. I had to politely explain that it wasn't *quite* what I had in mind and suggested that we go over the master tape again now, and I would tell him which bits I wanted in the film.

It took us about 30 minutes to pick out the bits I wanted, and he said that it would only take him about 40 more minutes to re-do it. When I said that I could wait 40 minutes, he looked at me oddly and said, 'Well, I can't do it right away, obviously. It's lunchtime.'

55

Monday morning, 12th September, and I was back in London for the presentation. I had finally got the video that I had originally asked for, and I had the one page of numbers from Claude. The four business heads were all to go into the boardroom separately to present our cases, and I was due to be the last in. This was a double-edged sword. On the plus side, it meant that Bernard would probably have got the bulk of his frustrations out of the way during the previous three presentations, but on the downside, he may well have lost the will to live by the time he got to me, and not hear a word I said.

The other three guys went in and came out, and I was trying to gauge the mood. Martin Cook, who ran the Bullings retail business was first, was in there for approaching two hours. He came out smiling but said that it had been quite a rough ride. He thought it had ended well though. The two Eastney Interiors leaders, Paul Newton in the UK and Rick Daniels in Florida both told a similar tale when they emerged, although neither of them was in for more than an hour.

When it got to be my turn, I walked in and sat down. Bernard and Fiona were talking quietly to themselves and either didn't see me come in or were ignoring me. Bernard then looked at me and said, 'Excuse me Peter, I need to make a call,' and left the room. So, they were ignoring me then...

After some small talk with Fiona, Bernard re-entered the room, sat down, and said, almost cheerily, 'Right, let's see what you've got to offer then.'

I talked through the numbers as quickly as I could, and the only comment came from Fiona who informed Bernard that the exit costs were lowest in France, mainly because all leases are on three-year terms in France, so the financial exposure was far lower than in the other businesses. When she said that, I wondered whether that was a good thing or a bad thing.

Moving as swiftly as I could onto the video, I just prefaced it by saying that this was a fair snapshot of what we were building in France and the people that were building it. I forgot to mention that I was slowly discovering a dark underbelly of 'them and us' within the teams that was going to take some further research on my part.

The video ran and there were no questions. Bernard actually laughed at the team singing in the Indian restaurant, which was at the end of the film. I was out in about 30 minutes, including Bernard's telephone call. His parting shot to me as I left the room, was, 'Peter, I need to make some difficult decisions over the next few days, and whatever comes from that, please understand that nothing's personal here.'

56

There being no point in my going back to France that night, I took the opportunity to spend a night at home. It was better to mope around with my long-suffering wife and dog, Garfield, than on my own in a hotel in Lille.

I don't share problems easily. I know many people whose first response to any disaster is to call someone to talk it through, but I don't. I much prefer to just take time to process things in my own head without any interference, or 'help' as some people insist on calling it. Kim knows this and just leaves me alone when she can see I need space. Garfield's way of helping, however, is to bring me his lead and look at me with the saddest of faces until I take the hint and go for a walk with him.

Bizarrely, I do share thoughts with Garfield while we walk, and that night, whilst in the fields that abut our home, I was telling him of the injustices of corporate life and how tough it was proving to get a business going in France. When I turned round to see if he was listening, I was greeted by a smiling dog that was staring me right in the eyes, squatting down and squeezing out an enormous stinking present to deal with. The irony of that moment was exactly what I needed. I gave him a big hug and smiled to myself all the way home. Problem now in perspective, move on.

57

Sean called me the next morning while I was driving to Paris. He had finally found a flat that he liked, and whose owner was gracious enough to allow Sean to pay him a monthly rent. The flat was in Sarcelles, which was near to Charles de Gaulle Airport and the A1, so it was easy for him to get to Lille and Paris, as well as collect friends and family that flew in to visit. The flat was fully furnished which meant that Sean could move in immediately. The upshot of this was that he needed a couple of days off to get himself sorted, and to fill in the various forms that he still needed to. I said that I would come up and let him buy me a beer to celebrate his moving, but he said, 'Not sure about that, I need all my money for the move.' Ever the Yorkshireman.

I told him how the presentation had gone but didn't mention the parting comment. There didn't seem much point and, to be honest, I'd only just found a way to deal with it in my own head and didn't really want to talk about it again. I had a similar conversation with Claude and then made a conscious decision to think about other things. Things like how we were going to get nine depots fully stocked, 54 people trained on systems that we *still* didn't fully have, and a business ready to greet customers, all in the space of under three weeks. It was going to need a Herculean effort and was not going to be helped by a significant sector of my workforce owning a watch that could only count to 35.

On the Thursday of that week, and with Sean back at work, I was in the office in Lille with him and Claude. The whole office was functioning reasonably well, with the turbo-strength industrial SIM cards that we had rented glowing red-hot from the heat of data being exchanged, calls being made and documents being printed.

We were planning the next two weeks in as much detail as we were able. We would have all the building blocks we needed from Monday 19th, in terms of stock, systems, Wi-Fi, people, marketing literature, cars, even down to the cash we needed for each depot's till. The only issue being that nothing was in exactly the right place and no-one could use the pesky depot computers except Sean and Yasmine.

We had said that we would open on 30th September, even though that was a Friday, the logic being that if we uncovered any operational disasters on Day One, we would have the weekend to sort them out. With the number of different bases to cover in the ten days preceding the opening day though, I was beginning to wonder if it was still a good idea. Then, in the middle of this planning session, and I use the term *very* loosely, the phone rang.

Since my meeting with Bernard, I had jumped each time my phone rang, both hoping it was him and praying it wasn't in equal measure. This time it was, so I walked out of the office to take the call.

After some small talk on his part, he said, 'Can you talk at the moment?' When I said that I could he told me that there was going to be an announcement to the city the next morning that he would be selling the Bullings retail business to the highest bidder and closing down the business in Florida.

I replied, *'Oh... and...?'*

'And nothing, don't you think that's enough to be getting on with?'

'Of course, sorry, so we can keep going in France?'

'Yes, it's close to home and we are going to need an alternative source of growth when the UK matures and it looks like we have a fighting chance in France, so don't let me down.'

'I won't.'

'You're doing well over there. Keep digging.'

'Thanks Ber...'

Click.

It took me about ten minutes to digest this news, which I did in my car alone. I then called Kim as I had said I would when I had an update, and then went back inside to share the news with Sean and Claude.

The news was met with a mixture of shock regarding Bullings and Florida, and relief about our own situation. I decided it was time to call an end to the day's meeting and that we should meet up in the Crest bar at 6.30pm when we would have had some time to digest it. I was also considering how best to communicate the news to my team, and when.

58

Given the relief that we were going to be allowed to pursue the French market, one would have thought that the evening would have been celebratory, but it was more one of reflection and thinking of the consequences both for us, and our good friends in Bullings and Florida. I couldn't call anyone yet as the announcement wasn't being made until the next day, and I didn't know who knew what at that stage, so we were left with many questions and no answers.

We wandered off to the Indian restaurant in Lille, and rather than dwell too long on the issues from today, it was time to move the conversation onto more important matters. So, over dinner, we discussed the extremely delicate subject of whether English cuisine was better than French cuisine. In hindsight I wish I had chosen a slightly less thorny debate, like whether left wing politics are better than right wing politics, or how best to fix Third World famine.

I drew that discussion to a close after an hour or so and, before blood was drawn, challenged Claude to find a French restaurant where the three of us could all leave saying that the meal had been fantastic. He accepted my challenge and that pleased me immensely as I genuinely wanted to find the holy grail of French food of which others frequently spoke.

59

The announcement was released at 7am London time the next morning, Friday, so I called Didier and asked him to get it circulated to the teams. Didier was interested in the situation, but no more than that. He said that as it didn't affect the French business and our team didn't really know anyone in Bullings or Florida, he didn't expect many questions. That made sense when I thought about it. No-one knew about the presentation I had given to Bernard or the angst that Sean, Claude and I had been through since, and so the news from London was '*just information*' as Didier described it.

60

The final two weeks before we opened were a blur. There was a sort of structure to it, but it was a case of there being more exceptions than rules. Sean and Yasmine were doing sessions on the point-of-sale system and the design system, which was occupying the very people that we needed to deal with the avalanche of stock that was arriving in every depot, seemingly simultaneously. Posters were going up, floors were being cleaned, and some fitters were busy finishing off kitchen displays in a couple of depots. And still, with all the jobs that needed doing in such a short time, many of the team would down tools at exactly their designated hour. It seemed that the fact that they had all had quite a bit of time off in recent weeks counted for nothing now. So much for '*give and take*'.

Slowly, piece by piece, the chaos started to look like a kitchen business. It wasn't perfect by a long shot. I had advised the teams where best to put particular products within their warehouses and it would do to get them going, but they were going to need to spend time making it the layout that they wanted. We managed to get basic systems training into the staff, to the extent that they could do an invoice and close up at the end of the day. The designers could provide a basic kitchen plan, but the online presentation side of it would have to wait a while. The safety signage was going up and the back offices in the depots were starting to look they could actually be a workplace for someone.

It was about 9pm when Sean and I got back to the hotel on Thursday 29th, the day before we opened. Claude had gone home for dinner as it was his wife's birthday, which left just the two of us to reflect on the previous six months. In one sense it had flown by in a heartbeat, but when we thought back to the first meeting we had with Madame Dupont in her office, it seemed like a million years ago.

We should have felt like having a party; after all, we had achieved the seemingly impossible. We had created a business of 69 people, nine depots, a head office and a distribution centre all inside six months. We didn't feel like partying at all though, partly because we were dead on our feet, and partly because we were both very nervous of what lay ahead. We had been told by just about everyone that our core customer didn't buy the products that we sold, and yet we had ploughed on regardless. Tomorrow was going to be the acid test of whether I had been right to tell Bernard that we should carry on a few weeks ago. I was minded of a quote by Helmuth von Moltke, stating that '*no plan survives first contact with the enemy*'. We had set up the business as a mirror image of the UK one, but we were going to need to be flexible and agile in adapting it to our customers' requirements in France. We had literally no idea what that meant at that stage, and it was more than a little scary.

PART TWO
TRACTION

61

Peter, Sean and Claude were an unlikely trio. Claude had the qualifications and experience in his field and was French, while Peter and Sean had been fumbling in the dark on this project from Day One; and were English. Even the two Brits had quite different upbringings. Peter came from a working-class family in Chichester, therefore making him a 'southern softy' in the eyes of Sean, who himself was from a well-to-do family in Harrogate and had traditional Yorkshire values. Peter would frequently rib Sean about his reluctance to part with any money, and at how few clothing layers he appeared to need, even in the coldest of climes. Claude would just roll his eyes at these two bickering about the smallest of things, even though he frequently made himself the target of their humour with his tendency to wear a big woolly scarf wrapped around his neck like a huge cravat the minute the thermometer went below ten degrees Celsius outdoors. He would even wear his enormous scarf indoors if it was chilly outdoors.

Despite that, these three compadres had learned to trust, respect and rely on each other. They even enjoyed each other's company – so long as the conversation didn't drift into culinary territory.

On Friday 30th September, Peter and Sean were going to spend time in as many depots as possible, thanking the teams for their hard work so far, but equally to remind them that the real work had only just begun. Claude, on the other hand, was going to spend the day in the Lille office, making sure that any support the depots needed was there for them.

Sean's day had started at about 7am, with the first of what turned out to be many telephone calls about how to use the computers. Even as Peter and Sean were checking out of the hotel, Sean was trying to do it with his phone wedged between his ear and shoulder, while still managing to be polite to the receptionist.

Check out completed, Peter and Sean parted company for the

day with a cheery wave and a shout from Peter that he hoped to hear from Sean later that day with a big fat sales figure. Sean meekly replied, 'Yes, me too…'

Peter's first stop was the closest one, the one at Lille that also housed the head office. He made a conscious effort to not go into the head office itself for fear of being sucked into time-consuming conversations that he didn't want to entertain that day.

As he walked in, he was greeted by a smiling Pierre, the manager of this depot.

'Hi Pete, good to see you.'

'You too Pierre, had any customers in yet?'

'No, but we are doing well putting the stock away and making plans.'

Pierre led Peter into the warehouse, where he was met by all the other staff members dutifully putting boxes into racks, including the external sales representative and telesales person who, by rights, should have been actively seeking new customers and sales.

'What's going on here Pierre? Those two shouldn't be doing that, should they?'

'Well, there's no-one here to serve yet, so I thought that they may as well work in the warehouse.'

'Umm, do you not think that the reason there are no customers is *because* those two are working in the warehouse instead of trying to create sales?'

This thought didn't seem to be on Pierre's radar at all, so he shrugged his shoulders and said, *'Well, the place is a mess at the moment, and we are working on our grand opening as well.'*

'Oh, OK, what time does that start?' asked Peter

'11am.'

'OK, well you'd better get yourselves organised then, that's only a couple of hours away.'

'Not 11am today; 11am on Thursday 27th October…'

Peter bit his lip as hard as he could without drawing blood, and after a minute or so said, 'Pierre, today is our grand opening day.

Today is when we start to sell products, not two weeks' time.'

'*But look at the mailout Pete, we are going to get a food truck in and have a raffle and create a great buzz for creating relationships.*'

'OK, so how many invitations are you going to send out?'

'*About one thousand.*'

'And how many of those do you hope to see on the day?'

'*Maybe one hundred.*'

'Right, so how many staff do you have?'

'*Six, including me.*'

'So why do you want one hundred people here, when you only have six people to talk to them?'

After a period of staring blankly at Peter, Pierre said, 'Well, they can talk to each other can't they, if we are busy, and anyway they can have a glass of wine while they wait.'

Peter was a little concerned by this. The issue of liability worried him, and if an accident occurred after his staff had been pouring wine into a builder, he didn't want to be incarcerated because of it. He said, 'Sorry Pierre, I can't let you have alcohol in the depot, not even for customers.' Pierre shrugged again, and said, 'OK, no problem.'

Peter finally managed to convince Pierre that the sales representative should be out in her car, and the business developer should be on the phone creating interest. Pierre said, 'But now there's only three people putting stock away,' to which Peter replied, 'What about you, can't you help?' Pierre looked horrified at this and said, '*Pete, I, am the manager.*'

62

Sean drove down to Paris, figuring that if there was going to be a torrent of phone calls, he could deal with them as well in a car as in a depot, besides which, he didn't want to be home too late that night as he had some friends flying in from Yorkshire for the weekend and he was looking forward to that. He arrived at Pantin, in the north-east of Paris, at about 10.30am and was met by a similar picture to the one Peter had witnessed, in that everybody was putting stock away. However, at least in this one the manager, Carlos from Portugal, was talking to what looked like an actual customer.

Carlos acknowledged Sean with a wave and carried on talking to his guest, so Sean walked through to the warehouse to chat to the others.

'Who is Carlos talking to?'

'It's his brother-in-law, who is a builder.'

'OK, well, that's a good start.'

'We've already had his uncle in this morning as well.'

'Big family then?'

'Seems so…'

Sean dealt with a few more phone calls about computers while Carlos finished with his brother-in-law, and then they had a walk round together.

'So, have you managed to sell anything yet today?'

'No. They will both take some flooring in a few days for jobs they are on, but they haven't got any kitchen business for us. My uncle fitted kitchens in Lisbon but hasn't since he arrived here ten years ago. My brother-in-law has never fitted a kitchen, but doesn't see why he can't as he has the qualifications for gas and electric that it requires.'

'What do you think we need to do to get them to buy a kitchen?'

'I've shown them how they can make some money doing it, so it's up to them now to see if anyone they know needs a kitchen sometime soon.'

With a similar conversation in Pantin as Peter had just had at Seclin about the use of sales representatives and telesales staff, Sean drove off to the next depot – the one at Meaux, to the east of Paris.

On the drive, Sean called Peter back. He had missed a few of Peter's calls as he had been answering questions about the systems.

'How's it going in Paris then?'

'Slowly, I've seen a customer in a depot though.'

'Brilliant, that's better than up here, I just had a bit of a falling out with Pierre in Lille. When I suggested he go into the depot and get his hands dirty with the troops, he basically said that it was beneath him.'

'You're being unreasonable again, aren't you?'

'It would appear so.'

After several more similar stories of how good things were going to be in each depot when they finally 'opened', came the end of the day's trading figures. Peter waited excitedly for Sean to phone through the sales figures and, at just after 5pm, the phone rang.

'Good day?'

'If a good day is judged by the number of questions I've answered about computers, it's been a brilliant day. By just about any other metric though, it's been poor.'

'Ok, what were the day's sales?'

'Zero.'

'Nothing? In nine depots?

'Nothing. We have opened ten credit accounts though, and four of those were to family and friends of the Turks and Portuguese teams who are in the trade.'

Peter paused a while, not out of some power game tactic, but out of genuine disappointment. After a few seconds, he raised as cheery a voice as he could muster and said, 'OK, a good start on accounts then, and we have to start somewhere. Well done for that and have a great weekend with your friends.'

Peter put the phone down and stared out of the window. He hadn't expected the builders to immediately beat the door down to buy kitchens, but he had hoped that they would sell *something* on Day One, and the depot staff not even considering that they had even opened yet clearly wasn't helping matters.

63

Sean picked his friends up from Charles de Gaulle Airport at 5.30pm that same day and, after dropping their bags off at his flat, they piled into a taxi and went into town. He needed a break from work; the previous six months had been pretty full-on, and the fact that they had opened today and sold nothing rested heavily with him. He had picked up the same vibe as Peter on his travels, the sense that until the French teams had gone through the process of a grand opening event, they didn't expect to have to deliver any tangible results. The Turks and Portuguese were at least getting on with contacting their own communities to get going, but even they were talking of open days and buffets.

To put it behind him, he was going to have a fun weekend with his two friends from Leeds University, John Banks and Harrison 'Harry' Richmond. When he said 'fun', what he meant was as much beer as possible, with the minimum amount of cultural exposure required to at least give John and Harry a plausible story of a sensible weekend when they got home to their respective partners on Sunday. To this end, Sean had planned a pub crawl, or at least the closest you can get to a pub crawl in Paris, based on the tour guide bus that does the rounds in most major capital cities. This appealed to Sean on a couple of levels. Firstly, it avoided too much logistical planning once on the bus, and, secondly, it was cheap.

OK, primarily, it was cheap.

That was tomorrow though; tonight was a much more basic night out. A few bars and then dinner at the Rib Rack Café, followed by a few more bars. They took the taxi to the area around the Imperial Hotel, as there was a Metro station there and it's far quicker to take the underground into the centre of Paris than a taxi. Also, there was McGuires, which was as good a starting point as any.

Aware of the fact that the business had only opened that day, John and Harry were keen to hear of Sean's stories. So, before Sean lost the capacity of reasoned discussion, he talked them through the toils so far, but only once they had a beer in front of them, which Sean made sure that he purchased. John and Harry both commented on how unusually willing Sean was to buy the drinks, and he just smiled and said, 'It's good to see you guys.'

Once settled, Sean began.

'Well, it's tough, I mean tougher than I expected, but we got there in the end.'

'So, what are the people like?' asked John.

'Good, my boss, Pete is a straightforward guy, a bit of a bull in a china shop at times, but a nice guy. We've got a French accountant with us who's great, but doesn't half go on, and the rest of the team are fine, well they're all French, so think differently to me, but we're getting there.'

'Well, you should be used to them by now, after your time here before. How's it going so far?' asked Harry.

'Crap, no sales today.'

'It was only the first day, so that's not surprising is it? It won't take you long to get builders to change suppliers,' said Harry.

'Builders in France don't buy kitchens.'

'What!?'

'Don't even go there, long story. Now drink up, there's a panoramic bar in the hotel opposite that gives a great view of the city and I thought we'd pop in there for one before going into town.'

The Tower Hotel was a place that Sean and Peter had used on occasions when the Imperial was full. It was a very tall hotel, 34 storeys tall to be exact, with a lobby bar in the general reception area, and a panoramic bar at the very top.

Once they had mastered the unnecessarily complicated lifts, they arrived in the bar and were immediately impressed with the beautiful view across Paris with the Eiffel Tower rising majestically as a centrepiece. While John and Harry were standing at the glass admiring the view, Sean sat down and picked up a drinks list. He called the waiter over and ordered three small beers, which were waiting for the other two when they had finished at the window.

'Did you ever bring Jane here?' asked Harry when seated.

'No, that's just another thing I regret really,' replied Sean.

'Do you regret that more, or less, than shagging her sister?' laughed John.

'Ho ho,' said Sean, 'very witty. I would say that shagging your sister-in-law is slightly worse.'

'Are you still in touch with her sister? Julie, wasn't it?' asked Harry.

'Yes, that's her, and no, I don't want to see her face ever again. That's a part of why I took this job to be honest.'

John asked, 'How is it with Jane since the divorce?'

Sean said, 'Well, I haven't really spoken to her to be honest. I've seen photos of her online out on the town recently in Leeds. I just hope she's happy – she deserves it.'

After a few more minutes, the beers were done and Sean was keen to get the Metro into town, so he passed the bill over to his friends and said, 'I don't know whose round it is, but it's definitely not mine.' Harry picked up the bill and couldn't believe what he was seeing. Three 25cl bottles of Kronenbourg came to 48 euros, before a tip. When he had regained the power of speech, Harry said, 'No wonder you got the drinks in over the road. Jeez, that works out to 32 euros a pint!', to which Sean smiled and replied, 'As I said, it's *great* to see you guys.'

A few bars later, they arrived at the Rib Rack Café in Boulevard de Sébastopol. Until then, it hadn't really dawned on John and Harry that they had come all the way to Paris, to just be taken to an American café that they could easily have eaten at in Leeds. When asked about this, Sean told them of the ongoing struggle that he and Peter were having in trying to find the perfect French meal, and the challenge that Peter had set Claude to find the food of their dreams. 'Until then chaps,' said Sean, 'I will just have to assume that we are currently in the finest eating establishment in Paris.'

Given their location, a hot topic of conversation over dinner was the conspiracy theories surrounding the death of Princess Diana.

Sean was among like-minded people here, unlike when he was with Peter and Claude, who usually mocked him. As the wine flowed, the theories became more outrageous and unlikely, but the more enjoyable for it.

The next day, they were up and ready to leave at about 9am. Sean had organised another taxi, but this time, just to the airport where a train would get them into the city centre. Harry, who was still bleeding at the wallet from his bruising in the Tower Hotel, was still dripping about his 'financial trauma', much to the amusement of the others.

First stop for the intrepid tourists was the Louvre. This was the only one of the attractions that Sean had planned to go into, and that was just so his partners in crime could report that they had seen the *Mona Lisa*. Most people's idea of visiting the Louvre would be several hours enjoying the vast array of treasures, but Sean could get to the *Mona Lisa* and out again inside 20 minutes, and that included time to take photos of the sea of people also taking photos of Da Vinci's classic.

Having completed the cultural aspect of their visit, Sean asked his friends what they thought of it. Harry said, 'Isn't the *Mona Lisa* small?' and John said, 'Thank God that's over, where's the bar?'

With the help of the big red bus, the three friends were also able to enjoy beers very close to the Arc de Triomphe, The Eiffel Tower, Notre Dame and Napoleon's resting place, Les Invalides. They also walked up the Champs-Élysées, where they squeezed in a light lunch. Sean asked his friends to choose where they ate, and they chose a brasserie where they could eat frogs' legs and snails, just to tick another box or two. Sean, whilst not opposed to the meals that his guests were tucking into, chose a burger with chips. John challenged Sean by saying that he was just a typical Brit abroad that wouldn't immerse themselves in the local culture. Sean rose to the bait and said, 'I don't think I am; I mean I've tried everything that the French have to offer, and it's okay, but that's all it is – okay, and they charge you as if they were all Michelin star chefs. As far as I can see there's a myth regarding the food here, and it relies on people like you going home and saying it was wonderful, when actually, if I gave that to you in Leeds you would just complain about how fiddly it was to eat. Here though, you talk about it in some romantic way as if it's a creation of genius. It's the Emperor's New Clothes story, people have to say the food here is fantastic if they aren't to be viewed as ignorant, but I'm happy to play the part of the little boy who just tells it as it is. It's not disgusting by any means, but there is far better food in the world than what's on your plate right now.'

John and Harry sat and listened to Sean's monologue politely and then Harry said, 'If you've finished prattling on, isn't it about time you got some beers in?' Sean looked at the menu for the prices, winced a bit, but ordered them anyway.

After lunch, and a few bus rides, bars and beers later, they made their way to where the evening's entertainment lie, the Moulin Rouge. Sean had been there before and had told Pete that it was over-rated, but Pete's reply to that had been, 'So that means you had to pay to get in then?'

Sean had booked a table for the 9pm show, so they visited a few bars and pubs nearby first. There were a couple of Irish bars in the area, and they found one that had an English football match on. At around 8.30, they made their way to the club, settled down and enjoyed the evening. They didn't drink too much in the Moulin Rouge itself. Not because of the prices, although Sean made it clear that he disapproved, it was because they'd had many, many beers during the day, and they had reached their capacity by that time, so one bottle of wine between them with dinner was sufficient.

The show at the Moulin Rouge was well received. John and Harry didn't quite know what to expect. They'd heard tales of the tacky side of shows like this, but they were both impressed with the professionalism and energy of the performance. Sean's unusual mind prompted him to remark during the rousing finale, 'I wonder how many times they've done the can-can?'

In the taxi back to Sean's flat, all three of them fell asleep, the full bellies of food and alcohol finally having their natural effect.

On the Sunday morning, they all awoke feeling a little the worse for wear, although none would admit it. Sean had factored this in and had bought the food needed for a proper English fry up. This is not as easy in Paris as you might hope, the main issues being bacon and sausages. There are a few British shops dotted around in the major cities though, so Sean had managed to secure the goodies required. There was no plan per-se, but Sean thought that after a walk to blow away the cobwebs, they would eat at around lunchtime.

The walk had the desired effect, and they stopped for a coffee and croissant in a nearby café. Harry and John were slightly amused by the number of locals who were enjoying a glass of pastis with their breakfast coffee, as if this was somehow different to them beating their way past the hordes at the *Mona Lisa* the previous day to get to their beer. Sean offered them each a pastis, being reasonably confident that they would both decline, and thankfully for him, they did.

After a hearty brunch back at Sean's, John and Harry packed their bags and Sean dropped them back at Charles de Gaulle. It was only on the drive back to his flat that his mind drifted back to the business. It was a mixed feeling for him, he was still proud that they had managed to get the business open on time, and with relatively few operational issues on the first day. On the other hand, he felt like he was on an assault course where he had just scaled a 20-metre wall with his bare and bloodied hands, just to land the other side and notice the 50-metre wall now before him.

64

Claude was first in the office on Monday morning. Of the 11 people that were permanently stationed at the Lille office, he had probably been the busiest over the weekend, with reams of reports to run, check and send out. These would all be automated in due course, but for now it was a very manual affair. The fact that there had been no sales in the previous week had no impact on the number of reports he had to generate – mostly saying zero.

Claude's idea of a good day was different to Peter and Sean's in several ways. They were driven by sales, whereas Claude was more interested in gross margin. They were driven by people and energy, whereas he was driven by accurate reporting and governance. The three of them shared a passion for the business as a whole though and dovetailed well.

Next in was Yasmine. She had been quite busy over the weekend as well, checking that everything on the systems side had been doing what it should have. There had been a couple of small failures, but nothing of consequence.

'Morning Yasmine.'

'Hi Claude, good weekend?'

'Yes thanks, busy with reports, but good.'

'Me too, did you speak to Peter or Sean over the weekend?'

'I spoke to Peter, he sounded fine. I think Sean was on a boys' weekend in Paris so I didn't bother him.'

'OK, what time is the meeting today?'

'11am, if I can get everything ready in time.'

'I hope we sell something today; I need to know if my systems can cope with it!'

At 11.10am, everybody that Peter wanted for the meeting was in the office, but only Sean, Claude and Didier were in the meeting room with him. 'Can you round them up please?' asked Peter.

'Yes, will do,' replied Claude.

What Peter meant by 'round them up' was to drag them into the meeting room immediately, by their hair if necessary. What Claude heard in the exact same words was to tell each of them that the meeting was about to start, let them gather all their various folders, pencils and notepads, then go to the coffee machine to get the essential drink, without which no meeting can possibly start.

When he finally had a full house, Peter began by thanking everyone again for their amazing work in getting the depots open, a feat that seemed impossible just six months ago. He then asked each of the department heads for a summary of where their department was at, and what their current issues were.

With no sales to discuss as yet, there weren't any new issues. Everybody appeared to be on top of things in Peter's eyes, at least for now anyway.

Peter then turned to Sean and asked, 'What are we going to do about this daft idea that the staff seem to have that they aren't really open until they've had some sort of grand unveiling, and therefore, they don't have to sell anything yet?'

Sean said, 'Well, it's a tough one, because they all verbally acknowledge that they should be selling stuff today, but their actions point towards the open day scenario that you just described. It's difficult to pin them down on it.'

Peter said to the room, 'Does anybody have a view or any experience on this situation?'

To which Henri replied, 'Well, there is the "Portes Ouvertes" mindset here that people traditionally buy into. It's no more than an open day, but it is very widespread so I can see why the teams are talking about having one. I guess they couldn't do it in time for today because of the last-minute panic to get open on time.'

'OK,' said Peter, 'If we've got to have one of these in every depot, can we push the managers to have it as quickly as possible please, and while we're at it, can you get the managers to quantify what they consider to be a good result from these events, in terms of sales on the day, new leads, and new credit accounts please Sean. I want to know, in advance, what each of the managers considers a *good day* to look like, and how much each event is going to cost us, and then we can decide if they are a good idea or not.'

'Will do,' nodded Sean.

'One more thing Sean, I heard someone somewhere planning to give the customers wine, so can we just put a stop to that please?'

'No problem,' said Sean.

Meeting concluded, Peter and Sean spent the remainder of the day planning some meetings and seminars for the next month or so to keep the energy levels up. During these deliberations, at about 2pm, Sean took a call from Ahmet at Nanterre depot. All Peter could hear was 'Brilliant, well done' about five times, so was eager to hear the story when the call concluded. Sean looked at Peter and said with a huge grin, 'We've only gone and sold something!'

'Fantastic news,' said Peter. 'What have we sold?'

'Some flooring to Ahmet's neighbour who's a builder. There's no margin in it as we had to drop the price to beat his current supplier, but sold it, we have!' replied Sean.

'That's just perfect. Tonight, we celebrate.'

65

At home that night, Claude was putting the children to bed, being ably assisted by Booboo, whose contribution was to jump on the children's beds and lick the faces that had only just been washed.

Job done, and now sat down on the sofa with Fleur and a glass of red with Booboo in his rightful position beneath his owner's legs, Fleur asked how Claude's day had been.

'Well, we sold some flooring today, so that's good I suppose. It was sold at cost price though, so I wouldn't call it a great day myself, but Pete and Sean were over the moon with it. I don't just mean happy, I mean ecstatic. Goodness knows what they'll be like if we ever sell a kitchen! Pete sent a note out to all the depots telling them about the sale and praising the manager to the rafters. It was only 200 euros for Heaven's sake.'

'Well, as long as he's happy, that's a good thing,' said Fleur. 'How was the meeting?'

Claude replied, 'It was fine for me, but Pete's a very direct person, he thinks and speaks in straight lines, there's no room in his life for if, buts and maybes. The trouble is, he's in France now and we don't think like he does and he struggles with it. He was getting wound up today over the depots all wanting to have a grand opening day, because in his mind they are already open. I can see where he's coming from, but... well, it's a very English attitude, shall we say.'

Why don't you sit Pete down and tell him?' said Fleur.

'I thought about that,' said Claude, 'but I decided against it. I might do it at some point, but for now, I think he needs to find a way through it himself, for his own benefit.'

66

Peter wanted to get all the managers together to have a celebratory dinner for the first ever sale of Eastney Intérieurs, but Sean quickly talked him out of it. Peter, unperturbed by this defeat, said that instead, they would both have a traditional French dinner tonight to celebrate the landmark event.

Le Bon Goût in the old town of Lille was a restaurant of about 60 covers, so it wasn't small, but it wasn't too large to be impersonal either. Peter had chosen it because of another recommendation, this time from Pierre, the manager of the Lille depot. It didn't look as stuffy as the restaurant where Sean had previously engaged in his tug of war, but it was certainly in the upper quartile in terms of ambience. The pair were led to their table by the head waiter, an impeccably dressed individual who looked like he had been doing this all his life.

With a glass of Champagne to start, both looked long and hard at the menu, and after two minutes of silent staring, Peter looked up and said, 'Ah, shall we go somewhere else?'

Sean laughed and said, 'No, we're here now, I'll give it a go if you will.' Between them, they established that it looked like they did a fillet steak, albeit in a cheese and onion sauce that didn't sound appealing to either of them. Also, further down the menu, they discovered some chips hidden away, these being served with a chicken cordon bleu, but this was no ordinary cordon bleu, it had a mushroom and leek crust. If they could somehow get the steak without the sauce, served with the chips from the chicken meal, this particular evening could be dragged from the jaws of defeat.

When Peter tried to explain what they wanted, the waiter simply said that the fillet steak was served with sauce, rosemary baked potatoes and seasonal vegetables. Peter said, 'Yes, I can see that, but could we please have it plain, and just with the fries that you serve the chicken meal with? So that's a simple steak, with fries. Is that possible?'

The waiter said, 'That's not the way chef likes to serve it sir, and he's been our chef for almost 20 years now.'

Peter, trying his hardest to be polite, but wanting to scream at this man that he was the damn customer, said politely, 'Do the meals arrive here frozen?'

The waiter was horrified by this question and started quoting the provenance of each of the products offered.

Peter said, 'Ok, if the food arrives here fresh, it is possible to present it in the manner I have requested, isn't it?' still somehow managing to maintain a calm demeanour.

The waiter made some notes, said, 'I will ask chef,' and disappeared.

The waiter walked through the swing door into the kitchen area, and within a couple of minutes, an almighty cacophony could be heard, with shouting, slamming and what sounded like an axe landing into a wooden chopping board. Peter said, 'This isn't looking good.' Sean, on the other hand, was just trying to avoid the gaze of the other guests in the restaurant who were staring at them, wondering what on earth had just happened.

Shortly after the noise subsided, the waiter emerged through the other swing door, walked straight across to Peter, said, 'That will be fine sir,' and walked off without further comment.

When their meal arrived, it was the plain steak and chips that they had asked for, but served in the middle of the standard issue, over-sized plate, and with an artistic swirl of red coulis circling, but not touching the food. Peter said, 'They just can't help themselves, can they?'

Sean replied, 'At least they didn't throw us out; let's call it a score draw.'

They agreed that the meal itself was fine; after all, it was just a steak and chips but, at the thick end of 40 euros per person, one would expect it to have been good. Peter commented, 'It's still not a patch on the steaks you can get in Florida.'

With all the fuss they had been through to get the meal they desired, the main reason for the event had been somewhat overshadowed, so Peter pulled it back on course by toasting the first sale of Eastney Intérieurs in France, and to there being many more to come. Sean said, 'We will probably remember today more for the fight with the chef in here than the flooring sale, do you think that's what they mean when they talk about French cuisine? It's not the food that's memorable, it's the arguments!'

Peter found this particularly amusing and during the meal they slowly drifted into a conversation about which two cars they would purchase if they had a budget of £150,000 and had to accommodate all driving situations. Peter opted for a fully loaded Audi Q7 and a hot hatch, like a BMW140, whereas Sean preferred to spend the lion's share of the budget on a sporty convertible like a Mercedes SL63 Roadster, and then spend any change on a cheap second-hand Land Rover. It was the utter futility of these discussions that appealed to both of them and kept their spirits up.

As they were settling the bill, the waiter whispered discreetly to Peter that, should they ever come back into this restaurant, the chef would be grateful if they could respect his menu.

As they were walking back to the Crest Hotel, Sean asked Peter what the waiter had said, to which Peter replied, 'He'd rather we didn't ever go back there.'

67

With life going on, but still no real energy in the depots until the open days had taken place, it was time for Peter to go to London to report at the executive meeting. When it was his turn to report, Peter was forced to explain to the committee, and Bernard in particular, the concept of the French depots being open yet not open until they had gone through their inaugural ceremonies. While the executives sat quietly during Peter's somewhat awkward summary, Bernard afforded no such luxury.

'Peter, who's in charge of that business, them, or you?'

'*Me.*'

'Are the depots all open now?'

'*Yes, but...*'

'If they are open, where are the sales?'

'*OK, point taken Bernard, leave it with me.*'

Tail very much between legs, and grateful that his contribution to the meeting was over, Peter sat quietly as Fiona gave an update on the proposed sale of Bullings and the closure of the US business. The closure in Florida would be effective at the end of December. Some key people were to be given retention bonuses to encourage them to hang around until the bitter end, particularly in HR and finance.

The sale of Bullings was a more complex affair, partly because the sales had been stagnant for some while, but mainly because some of the details surrounding the leases were complicated and expensive to deal with. This led to people trying to cherry pick the stores they wanted, which was something that Bernard was trying to avoid.

Peter consoled himself on the way back to Lille that afternoon that at least he wasn't the only one having sleepless nights. He did, however, really need to inject energy into the French business to get these openings out of the way, put some sales through, and hear those tills ringing.

68

Sean, by a combination of coercion, encouragement and small amounts of threatened violence, finally managed to create a sheet detailing exactly when the open days were going to take place, what the proposed event included, the estimated costs for the day and what each manager expected from the day's activity. He then gave it to Claude to create a tidier spreadsheet and circulate.

'Jeez Claude, that was like pulling teeth. Why is it so difficult to get these guys to give a straight answer to a straight question?'

Claude replied, 'That's actually a deeper question than you probably have the time or patience to deal with right now. Why don't we have a beer one night and I'll try to give you some pointers in what makes a French person tick.'

'Christ mate, if you can do that, I'll buy you a whole barrel of the stuff. Well... on expenses, obviously.'

'Yes, obviously,' chuckled Claude.

69

It was now Monday 24th October, they were three weeks in, and still no kitchens had been sold. There had been dribs and drabs of flooring sales and some odd bits of mastic and screws here and there, but no actual kitchens. The designers had been creating imaginary kitchen designs and quotes as mailshots to give an indication of the services and earning opportunity available, and this had resulted in six requests for designs across the nine depots. *This* week, however, thought Peter, was going to be different. *This* was the week that all the depots were having their *grand banquets*. *This* was going to be the week that got the business out of the starting gates. At least that was what got Peter out of bed at 4am on that Monday morning.

Peter had shared with Kim that he expected good things this week from the depots, and this earned Peter a muffled 'good luck' from somewhere under the duvet as he left the bedroom.

The open days weren't all on the same day. There was one today, in Versailles, and Peter wanted to get down there to see the event for himself. He arrived at about 11am, and Sean was already there. Miguel, the manager, was busy talking to a young couple who were setting up a large barbecue in the car park. Miguel was a friend of Carlos, the manager of Pantin depot and he had his roots in Portugal as well.

'I'm looking forward to this Miguel,' said Peter.

'Me too Pete, I'm expecting around 120 people.'

Peter suppressed the urge to remind him he only had six staff to deal with the flood of people expected, and said, 'That's great, do you mind if I stick around for a while?'

'Of course not, it's good to see you here.'

Peter and Sean bunkered into one of the back offices where they could see what was going on without being in the way. They were going through the spreadsheet that Claude had created with each of the managers' forecasts for their open day. Miguel had forecasted sales of 5,000 euros, ten new kitchen quotes, and ten new customer credit accounts. 'Well,' said Peter, 'let's hope the people that have said they will arrive, actually do,'

Sure enough, at around lunchtime, a few people started to arrive. These weren't the sort of builders that Peter was used to seeing, these were well-dressed businessmen and women. Miguel and his team were busy showing the guests around and offering them a coffee or a cold drink. Peter was sure that he could see a few bottles of wine on one of the tables and said to Sean, 'You did tell them about having no alcohol at these events, didn't you?'

Sean said, 'Absolutely I did.'

'So,' said Peter, 'what do you think is in those bottles on that table over there then?'

'Little buggers, leave it with me,' said Sean and he was halfway across the car park in a heartbeat and managed to grab Miguel. Peter could see that there was a quite lengthy discussion taking place, and upon his return, Peter asked what the story was. 'Well,' said Sean, 'you're not going to believe this, but when you said no alcohol, they didn't really bat an eyelid, because they only ever planned to serve beer and wine, and that beer and wine aren't termed alcohol. He said they specifically use the word 'alcohol' for things like whisky and brandy. You know, the 40-odd percent stuff.'

A quick phone call to Claude confirmed this to Peter, and he decided to let it be, rather than cause a fuss today. By now, the car park was very busy, there were indeed many people hanging around chatting to each other and the staff. The barbecue was at full pelt with smoke bellowing across the car park and onto the adjacent road. This merely gave Peter something else to worry about, so he and Sean waved a cheery goodbye to Miguel and looked forward to getting the sales figures later that day.

When out of earshot of the depot, Peter said, 'I should have stopped the barbecue and the drinking really.'

Sean said, 'Maybe, but they are much more relaxed about certain things over here compared to the UK, and the consumption of wine with lunch is one of them. They even gave their troops a daily wine ration in the First World War.'

With some minor adaptations to the rules, Peter allowed the beer and wine to be offered at the open days. He instructed that nothing was to be poured into peoples' glasses, so that everybody was clear about how much they had consumed. If they wanted another drink, they would have to take a fresh glass from a tray that was placed on the depot counter. Peter convinced himself that this was the responsible thing to do, to allow the French to be French, while hopefully enabling him to get some sleep at night.

70

Peter couldn't wait for the 5pm figures to come that night, so he called Miguel at 4.30pm to ask how the day had gone.

'Brilliant Pete, we had a great day.'

'Excellent, what were the day's sales?'

'Oh, there were no sales, we were all too busy talking to customers to sell anything.'

'Too busy to sell anything? Surely that was the whole reason for doing the day?'

'Oh Pete, you should have seen it, there were people everywhere, chatting and enjoying themselves. Loads of people said that they will let us quote for some kitchens, it was fantastic.'

'OK, how many surveys did you book in the diary then?'

'None, but they will all come back, they promised.'

After this exchange, Peter reflected that it was a good job that he was at the Imperial and not closer to the centre of Paris at that moment, because right then he felt like walking to the middle of Pont Neuf on the River Seine and jumping off, particularly if he had Miguel as ballast.

That evening in McGuires, Sean and Peter were comparing notes on the day's performance at Versailles.

'How much did it cost us?' asked Peter.

'About 1,000 euros all told,' replied Sean.

'One thousand euros out, with precisely zero return – whoopee doo.'

'Well, in tangible terms, yes, but we did see a lot of people there, and that must count for something.'

'Maybe, but what gets me is when you look at the big picture. France is a hugely efficient economy in that the GDP is about the same as the UK. But there seems to be a massive disconnect between that headline and the story of day-to-day life. We've got suppliers making it difficult to buy, restaurants that value their menu more than their customers, staff that only want to work 35 hours a week, and a population that completely downs tools in the summer. What the hell am I missing here? How does this damn country work?'

'*Better men than us have pondered that thorny question over the centuries Pete.*'

'Is that supposed to make me feel better?'

'*Just trying to help...*'

'Well, help by getting your round in.'

'*Will do. By the way, I had a similar conversation with Claude a while ago, and he said that he'd spill the beans about how the French tick over a beer one night. That might shed some light on it I suppose.*'

'Yes, it might, but over a beer might not be the best way to do it. He waffles on at the best of times, and this will send him into overdrive. If he's got a beer in front of him as well, I think my ears may explode. We'll go up to the office tomorrow to talk to him.

71

'It depends what you mean by *understanding the French*,' was Claude's opening gambit.

'Forget it. If we need a five-hour debate to even understand what the bloody question is, I'm out of here,' snapped an unusually tetchy Peter.

He and Sean had driven up to Lille together on the Tuesday morning, leaving one car at the Imperial. There were two more open days happening today, one in Nanterrre, the depot managed by Ahmet from Turkey, and one in Englos, a depot near Lille that was managed by a Frenchman named Louis.

Sean had been speaking to both managers on the phone during the journey, and with both telling a similar tale to the one they had heard yesterday from Miguel, Peter was noticeably quieter during the journey than Sean was used to. He didn't even seize the opportunity to berate the two managers from his passenger seat on these hands-free discussions, instead choosing to just stare out of the side window at the somewhat desolate landscape that borders the A1 both sides between Paris and Lille.

'*It must have been hell,*' said Peter, about half way along the journey.

'What?' asked Sean.

'*Life in the trenches during the war, I mean just look at it, it's depressing enough now, let alone being under constant fire from the enemy as well. Have you noticed how many small cemeteries there are along this road? It must be in the hundreds.*'

'Yes, it's a similar story all around here, it's awful to say, but you get a bit desensitised to it after a while. There are many dedicated to the British, and to other Commonwealth countries as well. There are even German ones, but they only have a cross as a marker rather than a headstone. It's a very sobering thought when you take time to think about it.'

'*Indeed.*'

When they arrived at the office, Peter and Sean said their hellos to everyone at their stations. They had both adopted the hand-shaking greeting for both males and females in their time in France, with Peter even visibly stepping back if a lady lunged in for a double cheek rub. 'Completely unnecessary and unhygienic' was his view of the centuries' old tradition.

Sean received a call from Ahmet while they were doing the rounds in the office, and it sounded to Peter like it was good news. His hopes were dashed though, when Sean revealed that he was just reporting that some builders had started to arrive and they were giving them a sandwich and some wine. 'So, no sales to report then?'

'No,' said Sean.

'Bastards,' muttered Peter under his breath.

So, it was with a rather negative view on France and its natives that Peter sat down with Claude and Sean in Claude's office and then barked at Claude the minute he opened his mouth.

'Calm down Pete, you can't expect me to unravel a nation in the space of five minutes, and more than that, it's all subjective anyway – my view may be different to someone else's. I can only tell it the way I see it.'

'Yes, of course, sorry,' said Peter. 'It's just that I've never experienced anything this frustrating before. What do I need to do to make this business work?'

'I'm not sure I can answer that Pete,' Claude replied, 'I said to Sean that I would give him some pointers about how to understand the French as a group of people, and if you think that might help, I'm happy to share my view on the matter. It is only my view though.'

'That's fine Claude, I'm open to any suggestions at the moment.'

'OK,' said Claude, 'I'll just grab a coffee.'

'Of course you will,' whispered Peter as Claude left the room.

72

'Well, let's start at the beginning,' started Claude.

'Please God no. Could I possibly have the precis of the extremely shortened version please? And then maybe just a three-line summary of that for good measure?' groaned Peter.

'OK,' said Claude, 'I will do my best.'

Peter reminded Claude what Bernard had said to him about his best maybe not being good enough.

'Well,' started Claude, 'the revolution changed the way the French viewed themselves, and I know you've heard about the effect that Haussmann had, but the quest to be "more equal" than the next man has been a national pastime over here since Napoleon was a boy, literally.

'Education was one way that people could differentiate themselves from others within the new regime, and that mentality still exists today. People are judged by their education, and even which schools they attended. All the top businessmen and politicians attended a *grand école*, much like your Oxbridge institution, but with probably more of a linear effect on their career path than Oxbridge. There is a direct link in French people's minds between qualifications and colleges on the one hand, and that person's position in society on the other. It goes even deeper than that though; with status, comes a tremendous sense of entitlement, and that fact materially affects a person's behaviour. Status can also be defined by someone's reputation. For example, in some of the chefs you seem to have upset so far, or your potential customers, and that sense of status and consequential entitlement within their own society runs incredibly deep. I would say it has a similar effect on a person's sense of self-worth as your honours system.'

'Ha,' said Peter, 'if we make this business successful, I shall be demanding a knighthood for Sean and I, and a *Légion d'honneur* for you.'

Claude said, 'I very much look forward to that, but I haven't finished.'

'Oh,' sighed Peter.

'Alongside that is the fact that historically, France has produced many famous philosophers, like Sartre, Descartes and Voltaire to name a few, and philosophy is still a core subject in schools here, just like history or geography. Students learn to look at issues from many different angles in accordance with historical thinkers, and this affects the way in which they answer your questions. You may think you've asked a straightforward question of someone, but they could easily have interpreted it differently and answered it in an apparently obtuse manner. They aren't avoiding your questions; they are just not answering them in the way that you are used to.'

73

'Beef Bourguignon,' shouted Fleur, as Claude stuck his head out of the study door to ask what was for dinner. 'Great, I'll be down in ten minutes.'

Claude finished the report he was doing for Fiona and had a quick look at the sales figures for the day; most of the depots had sold bits and pieces, but there were no large sales. He then closed his laptop, that being his definition of ending his working day, gave Booboo a belly rub for sitting nicely under his desk for the duration, and went downstairs.

Over dinner, Fleur asked Claude how his day had been. Claude replied, 'Very well, I think. I had an hour or so with Pete and Sean today to give them a bit of help with understanding life in France.'

Fleur said, 'You said you were going to let him work it out for himself.'

'Yes, I know, but he asked directly, so I couldn't really say no, could I?'

'No, I guess not,' said Fleur. 'So, how did he take it?'

'Very well I think, he listened to everything I had to say, made some notes and we laughed about the differences between us, and I think it all made sense to him... Yes,' he said, making light work of the delicious meal that Fleur had prepared, 'I really think that they are starting to come round to our way of thinking.'

74

'Bloody idiot.'

'*Not avoiding the question,* my arse,' said Peter over their curry in Lille that night. 'What a load of old tosh.'

Sean chuckled, 'Yes, it's difficult to misinterpret the question *how many builders have you spoken to today*? isn't it?'

'Absolutely it is, unless you really haven't got a clue of course, in which case it must be very useful to have centuries of philosophy to fall back on.'

During a thoughtful period over the dinner, Peter said, 'There is something in what Claude said today though, he mentioned the builder's reputation and status, and while that applies everywhere to an extent, if the revolution has added weight to the intangible aspects of society, maybe we should try to push that aspect more over here, possibly even more than price or availability. After all, our entire business model is about making builders look good, so maybe we need to do better at promoting that here.'

Sean agreed, although his attention was mostly taken up by a particularly pleasant tandoori chicken leg.

'Anyway, any good news from the coal face today?' asked Peter.

'Potentially, yes,' replied Sean, 'we may well have our first proper kitchen going out tomorrow.'

'Great,' said Peter, 'what's the story?'

'It's at Versailles depot and is one of Miguel's family who's a builder. He's fitting a kitchen for the first time, so we are going to work closely with him to make sure it goes well.'

'Yes,' said Peter, 'I suggest you make him your new best friend.'

'Let's gather the guys at Suri's next week sometime if the kitchen does indeed go out. It will be good to celebrate it,' said Peter.

'OK, good idea,' replied Sean.

That evening's light-hearted discussion was to name their three favourite recording artistes of all time, in no particular order. This was a relatively argument free debate as there was no requirement to convince the other party that you were correct, so after much toing and froing, Peter settled on The Jam, Madness and The Fratellis, while Sean opted for Led Zeppelin, David Bowie and The Beatles. Peter couldn't help but quietly tease Sean about there having been some quite good music after 1985 if he dared to actually listen to any of it, but if Sean did hear him, he chose to ignore it.

75

Wednesday 26th October 2010 was a date that was to be etched in Peter's mind forever. It was the day that Eastney Intérieurs finally sold a kitchen in France. More than three weeks after they had opened, and with all of the grand opening events now behind them, a builder had finally been convinced to buy a kitchen. He was the uncle of Miguel, the manager of the Versailles depot.

The kitchen design had been checked three times before the invoice was created, including once by Sean, and the pallet of products had been checked four times, including once each by Sean and Peter. They were determined that kitchen number one would be problem free. They couldn't do much about any fitting issues that arose on site until they happened, but they could certainly make sure that there were no supply problems on the day.

Monsieur Barboza, Miguel's uncle, was most impressed with the service he received when he collected his kitchen. To be fair, it would be impossible to feel otherwise. There were seven people from Eastney Intérieurs there, including the two Brits. He couldn't help but notice that even though there were seven people present, only two of them were actually loading the kitchen onto his van. The rest were either chatting among themselves and staring, or in the case of the two Brits, photographing and videoing the event. On top of that, he was presented with a bottle of Champagne by the president of the company and given a bunch of flowers for his wife. Yes, Monsieur Barboza was being treated like royalty, Peter observed. To which, Sean replied, 'I hope not, they had a rather unique way of dealing with royalty, and so far, he's our best customer!'

76

It was a celebratory feel to the curry in Suri's the following night, Thursday. Sean had gathered all nine of the managers, and Peter had invited Claude, Didier and Henri. It was time to get some stories of their efforts so far; what was showing signs of promise, and what looked like it wasn't working yet. With just over a month of trading, and one full kitchen sale in the bank, it was time for a debrief.

Peter had told Sean, Didier and Henri that there were to be no negative comments about anything the managers said, only positive comments about the successes. Some depots had started better than others, but Peter didn't want anyone being singled out as failures at this early stage. As Peter put it, 'We are going to give water and sunlight to the successes so that they can spread into the more fallow areas of the business.'

Claude said, 'Very philosophical Peter, I like it,' whereas Sean whispered to him 'Who are you, and what have you done with Pete?'

Before the evening descended into a wine-fuelled singalong, Peter asked each of the managers to talk about what had been working well in their depots, and what the early customer feedback had been. He was given a fairly consistent story of a very positive response from the builders, and that the issue, if indeed there was one, was more to do with the lack of a natural connection between the builder and the end-user with regard to kitchens. Home owners didn't think about turning to their builder when they wanted a kitchen, and anything we could do to improve that situation could only make things better. Most of them mentioned doing some sort of retail-style advertising, and while this wasn't something Eastney had traditionally done in other markets, Peter didn't want to appear negative about this point over dinner, so just noted it politely.

Henri asked a general point of the table. He could see from the sales that we hadn't sold any of the blinds that Peter had insisted on stocking, but he was interested to know if it was a product group that the builders had been interested in when they were in the depot. The question prompted a stony silence from around the table, until Pierre from the Lille depot finally piped up, 'It's a made to measure product normally, none of my customers have mentioned them.' The ensuing mumbling in agreement from around the table told Henri all he needed to know, but he said nothing, and didn't look at Peter for any reaction.

Peter was watching how much of the Indian food people were taking. He had specifically ordered mild dishes this time around, except for Claude who had made a point of asking for the hottest dish they had. Overall, there was a better take up this time, with most of the team being slightly more adventurous. Peter said to Claude, 'You see, I'm grinding them down slowly.'

Claude replied, 'At least they are trying new things, unlike some people I could mention.'

'I'm still waiting for this gastronomic treat that you are going to put before me,' retorted Peter.

'Fair enough, I'm on the case,' said Claude, with a tone that suggested that he had forgotten all about that little challenge.

With the main course finished, and most of the entourage enjoying coffee and digestifs, Peter asked the table for quiet. 'Right then, to get this party started properly, I'll stick some money on the table for you to potentially earn. Let's keep it simple, the first manager to sell kitchens to ten different customers will earn an extra three months' bonus. The second manager to sell kitchens to ten different customers will earn an extra two months' bonus, and the third will earn an extra one months' bonus. The only caveats being that the kitchens must be over 2,000 euros each, and this offer lasts until the end of November. What do you think of that?'

Peter was used to offering extra bonuses in this manner; he had learnt that extra incentives around a dinner table with a small number of people had good impact. When he had done this in the UK and in Florida, there had been whoops of gladiatorial joy, with people getting on their phones immediately, making things happen. In Paris, on that evening though, he saw a different reaction. Instead of the cheering and banging on tables that he was expecting, the table went almost silent, sheepish even. Quite perplexed by this, he asked the table if they thought it was a good incentive, and again, he got a quite different reaction to the one he was expecting. His previous experiences told him that a few people would be quite loud in declaring that they were going to take the money off the table. Experience also told him that the loud ones were rarely the ones that actually took the money, but it always added to the energy of the evening, and that was a good thing in itself. Rather than make any rash commitments, Louis from the Englos depot, near Lille, quietly piped up, 'It would be good to achieve that.'

Peter, biting his lip and mindful of the instructions he had given the others about there being no negative comments, made a cheery comment and wished them good luck with the incentive. He paid the bill and left after a few more minutes, preferring to not be with such lacklustre individuals that didn't snap his arm off for the extra money. He told Sean to pick up the tab for any further drinks, and that he would see him tomorrow in the Nanterre depot.

As he walked back to the Imperial, he thought to himself, 'What on earth do I have to do to get these guys excited about the business?' It was a thought that stopped him sleeping well that night.

77

A grumpy Peter bumped into Sean in the lobby of the hotel on the Friday morning. 'How did it go after I left?' asked Peter.

'OK, we just had one more drink and left,' said Sean.

'Could you get any more energy out of them than I managed to?'

'Not really, they did ask if there could be some extra bonuses for the staff though.'

Peter thought for a few seconds and asked, 'So, you think they would rather have an equal payment structure than have it all themselves, to play to their egalitarian values?'

Sean said, 'No, I didn't get that sense at all, I think they want the big numbers that you offered for themselves, but some extra incentives for the staff to help them achieve it on top of that.'

'What?' ranted Peter, 'The whole point of paying the managers the big bucks is so that *they* make *their* staff work harder. If I've got to pay the staff extra money to do the jobs they are already paid to do anyway, I don't need to pay the managers do I?'

'Okay okay,' said Sean, smiling, 'don't shoot the messenger.'

On his way to Nanterre, an already despondent Peter had his mood lowered even further by a call from Claude. 'Hi Pete, I just wanted to run through that incentive you offered last night.'

'What about it?' snarled Peter.

'You do realise that we hadn't budgeted for that, don't you? And as we aren't even hitting the sales forecasts we gave Fiona before we opened, it is going to have a big impact on the P&L... oh and don't forget the social charges.'

'What about the social charges?'

'Well, they add 45 per cent to the cost of anything you pay people.'

'Yes, yes I know, is there any good news?' Peter asked.

'There is,' declared Claude excitedly, 'I've chosen a restaurant that I think you and Sean will like.'

'Mmm, I'll ask you again...'

78

With a weekend of pondering and talking things through with Garfield on his long walks through the woods, Peter decided to get Sean and Claude together again on Monday at Lille to discuss how they were going to jump start the business in France. The incentives in their current form didn't look like they would create the buzz that he had anticipated, and the way that sales were going meant it wouldn't be long before Bernard started making some changes in France. It was lucky for Peter that Bernard was busy with the sale of the Bullings stores.

More pressing than that for now though, was an action group that Kim had enrolled in, and a meeting that Peter had been roped into going along to on Sunday afternoon in the name of support. It was something to do with a community hall that the local authority had announced would close down shortly, and that Peter barely knew existed. Kim was friendly with the manager of the hall, and so Peter had become an unwitting participant by default.

They arrived at 4pm, 30 minutes before the meeting started, and Peter was forced to drink tea and make small talk with people who shared Kim's view on the planned closure. He was actually quite interested to hear what the plan for the land was after it had been bulldozed, but decided that this group of people were probably not the best to ask.

After 30 minutes of excruciating small talk about the hall and the events that they would be losing through its demise, he was able to sit down and listen to the arguments against the closure.

The table facing the audience seated six people; the committee, Peter assumed, and the first speaker was a very well-spoken and articulate lady named Jennifer Kingston. She started by welcoming the audience, a group of about 20 people Peter estimated, and moved on to the agenda for the meeting. They would be discussing their legal options, their social media options, and their more physical protestation plan. Peter's agenda was to say nothing, agree with everything and get out of there as quickly as possible.

He found himself actually getting interested in the plan, not particularly because Jennifer was a good orator, although she most certainly was, and not because he had suddenly discovered a latent affection for the community hall. It was more because her style was to make sure that everybody felt they were a part of the problem. She did this by asking rhetorical questions like, 'Can you honestly say that you have used this hall each time you could have?' and 'Have you recommended this hall for functions every time you had the opportunity?' By casting the responsibility for the current dilemma across the whole audience, she created the unspoken obligation for everyone present to be an active part of the solution. There was no blaming of local councillors, ranting irrationally, or trying to re-invent the wheel with Ms Kingston, she focussed very much on what could reasonably be done with the resources available, and then broke the overall task down into bite-sized chunks that everybody there could very likely commit to.

It would be a lie to say that Peter left the room as a community hall activist, but he did leave the room slightly more interested in the cause. Kim had agreed to set up the team that was going to parade outside the town hall with placards. Peter said, 'I never knew that I had married such a militant!'

To which Kim smiled and replied, 'Next stop, Westminster!'

Peter spent the rest of Sunday evening thinking about whether there was some mileage in Jennifer Kingston's approach. What if he could make the builders in France believe that they were the solution to his problem...

79

'Morning,' called out a cheery Claude as Sean walked into the office on Monday.

'Hi Claude,' replied Sean, 'how was your weekend?'

'Oh, could have been better,' said Claude, 'I had to spend most of it at the in-laws. It was their 50th wedding anniversary.'

'Ouch, sounds painful,' said Sean.

'It was, how about you?'

'Not bad actually, I went out with a few of the people in my neighbourhood yesterday. Just a walk and a spot of lunch, but it was good to meet some different people and not spend the whole weekend thinking about work.'

Claude laughed and said, 'It sounds like you're turning into a proper Frenchman!'

Sean turned his eyes to Claude without moving his head and said, 'I'll pretend you didn't say that.'

'Ha, I'll have you wearing a scarf like mine before you know it! Have you spoken to Pete this morning?'

'Yes, he's running late, the tunnel is slow today. Maintenance work has shut one of the tunnels apparently.'

Claude and Sean spent the time waiting for Peter to arrive going through the previous week's figures and trying to find some positives. Account recruitment was increasing nicely, and the number of kitchen quotes given to builders was quite respectable, especially given the fact that builders, historically, hadn't ever bought kitchens. It was just that last step, where a quote turns into a sale that the whole thing was coming to a grinding halt.

Equally as concerning was the fact that they had already started to lose sales to competitors. When Sean was reading the feedback from the managers, and indeed the customers, about why this was, the usual reply was 'the builder's customer decided to go elsewhere.' They weren't citing the price, the quality, the range available, or the service – all of the things that they could do something about. It was always the end-user's decision, something that was apparently out of their hands.

'Hmm, nothing's ever anybody's *fault*, is it?' said Sean.

'Sorry?' said Claude.

'Nothing,' replied Sean, 'just thinking out loud.'

80

After Peter had shaken everybody's hand in the head office and finally arrived at Claude's desk, he sat himself down and said, 'That, was not the start to the week that I wanted. Four bloody hours to get through the tunnel. Four!'

'Coffee?' asked Claude, as if it were the answer to any issue imaginable.

'Yes please,' said Peter, and they made their way into the meeting room.

Claude gave a summary of the previous week's financial performance, and Sean gave a summary of the operational matters. Peter sat quietly throughout, paying particular interest to Sean's observations about the sales that they were already losing.

When they had both finished, Peter told them of his idea to talk to the builders in small groups to see if they could get better engagement with them. He also said that it might be a good idea to do the same with the depot staff in the absence of the managers. He said that they might get a different story from the team when they were out of earshot of their boss.

Sean said, 'Righto, let me get on with it.'

Peter replied, 'I don't think that you or I are the right people to do this. *We* have an English idea about tackling problems, and I want to hear what the *French* ideas are. I thought we could get Claude, Didier and Henri to take a couple of groups each. Is that OK with you Claude?'

'Absolutely it is, I'll speak to the other two and we'll get something organised for next week.'

Peter said, 'Sorry Claude, I want answers by Friday of this week, you're going to have to get on with it, like, this minute.'

'Oh, alright then, *permission to leave the room Sir*?' said Claude in his most military like voice.

'Granted,' smiled Peter. 'Oh, before you go Claude, when shall we try the restaurant you suggested?'

'Thursday night okay with you two?' asked Claude.
'Perfect,' said Peter, 'looking forward to it already.'

81

During the course of the next few days, Peter and Sean carried on visiting the depots, asking pretty much the same questions wherever they went and getting pretty much the same replies. They did see a few more kitchen sales go through that week, albeit at shockingly low gross margins, but Peter consoled himself that they had to start somewhere, and until there was a volume of sales to discuss, any conversations about margin were just a distraction.

They stayed in Paris for two nights that week; the threat of French food on Thursday subconsciously drawing them to Suri's to stock up on good food, like a squirrel stashing its nuts.

'So, tell me more about these neighbours of yours then,' asked Peter over an onion bhaji.

'Nothing to report really, it's just a group of people that go out walking together at weekends if the weather's okay, and the lady in the village shop invited me along as I'm new to the area.'

'Lady in the village shop, eh?' enquired Peter, mischievously.

'Yes, the lady in the village shop,' replied Sean in a very matter of fact tone.

'Does the lady in the shop have a name?' asked Peter.

'Yes, Colette,' answered Sean, '...and her husband's name is Jean-Claude.'

Moving onto more comfortable territory, Sean started the conversation ball rolling again with a question about what their last three-course meals would be if they were facing the firing squad the next morning.

'...or a breakfast meeting in London,' laughed Peter.

82

'Speak of the devil,' said Peter as they were driving together on the *périphérique* the next day. He put the phone to his ear and said, 'Hi Bernard, how are you?' Sean was conscious that Peter was quiet for a longer time than normal when speaking to Bernard during the call, and apart from a few comments of 'ok' and 'fine', he said nothing. When the call had finished, Peter didn't say anything, and Sean didn't ask.

After a few quiet minutes, Peter said, 'He's sold Bullings.'

'OK,' said Sean, 'that's good, isn't it?'

'Well, yes,' started Peter, 'but he hasn't got anything like the price for it that he wanted, and so some of the things that he was going to spend that money on, he now can't.'

'Does that impact us at all?' enquired Sean.

'Well, it wouldn't if we were hitting the numbers that we said we would, but he said he can't afford little luxuries like us if he's got less money to play with. Basically, we've got to get the P&L back to where it should be, and in double quick time.'

'Or what?' asked Sean.

'He didn't say… and I didn't feel like asking.'

83

Thursday night finally arrived, and Peter and Sean were in the Crest Hotel at Lille, waiting to be picked up by Claude in a taxi. Having bellies full with two nights of Indian food, the interlopers were feeling less vulnerable than normal.

'Right then, do your worst,' was Peter's greeting as they entered the taxi.

'That's what I like to see, an open mind,' said Claude in response.

'So, where are we off to then?' asked Sean.

'Aah, just you wait and see,' said Claude.

Very shortly after setting off from the hotel, Sean observed that they were entering Belgium. The irony of this was not lost on the tourists. 'So, Claude, let me get this right, the best food in France, is, in your opinion, in Belgium,' said Peter, with a grin as wide as a Mexican hat.

'I knew you'd be like this,' said Claude, 'but I still think the best way to indoctrinate you into the finer foods available in my great country, is to start you off in a place like the one we are going to. All I ask is that you give it a fair chance.'

'Of course,' Peter said, but the rest of the journey was made up of Peter and Sean ribbing Claude about how the business might be easier to run if it was in *this* bit of France, and Claude studiously ignoring them.

About 30 minutes later, they arrived at the restaurant, it was called Chez Lambert in Tournai, and had the feel of being in a large wine cellar. They were greeted by the owner on arrival, Monsieur Lambert, and it was clear to the Brits that Claude was a regular here, with Monsieur Lambert asking him about how Fleur and the children were.

They were shown to a corner table where they could talk fairly privately, and three glasses of Champagne arrived within a couple of minutes. Shortly after that, the menus arrived and they immediately dived into them to see what delights lurked within.

They were able to choose quite quickly from the fairly limited choice available and were then able to discuss how Claude's interviews with the staff and customers had gone.

'To be honest Pete, I did the staff. Didier and Henri did the customers and I won't get their views until tomorrow morning. If you could drop by at around lunchtime, I should have it all ready for you.'

Peter said, 'OK, that's fine, did the staff drop any bombshells?'

Claude said, 'Not in the sense that I think you're after, in that none of them came up with an idea that is going to make things perfect overnight. They did mention concerns about all of the focus being on the managers, and that they would like a bigger slice of the action, like the trips and bonuses – that sort of thing.'

'Yes, I get that,' said Peter, 'but the idea is that the business is focussed on the managers, and we want the staff to aspire to be managers. The trips and bonuses come with the responsibility to deliver a successful business, and you can't really have one without the other, but I do get what they are saying.'

Sean added, 'Maybe our way isn't egalitarian enough for France.'

Peter replied, 'I'm starting to think that *égalité* is a French urban myth to be honest. What I'm seeing is a group of people that want it all for themselves, just so long as no-one else sees them getting it.'

With the wine having been chosen by Claude, the trio waited with anticipation for the meals to arrive. Claude was already trying to lower his friends' expectations of the evening, a point that was not lost on his audience. He wasn't going to be allowed to wriggle out of this one if his guests were to have anything to do with it.

The food arrived and was placed before them. Peter had chosen the salmon, Sean the chicken, and Claude the steak. All three meals were presented simply, but with care. There was none of the artistic creations and 'jus' that they had become used to in France accompanying their meal, nor was it covered in foam and on a huge plate. It was just food, presented well.

All three finished their meals, giving Claude the answer to his next question before he had even asked it, but he did anyway. 'Well? What do you think?'

Sean answered first by saying, 'That, was very good food Claude, but we can't overlook the fact that we are not actually in France, can we?'

He replied, 'No, but you see, what you refer to as *French food*, is just this, but with more bells and whistles. Okay, maybe a bit of pomposity as well for good measure, but if you look through all of that, you are left with food that is as good as the food you have just eaten.'

The jury was out on that one as far as Peter and Sean were concerned, but neither wanted to offend their friend and colleague after such a valiant effort.

The conversation over coffee and digestifs was a question tabled by Claude. 'Right guys, Napoleon – hero or villain?' The verdict was surprising to Sean and Peter, as they both decided that if it had to be a binary answer, they would choose hero. Claude, on the same understanding of it needing to be a binary answer, opted for villain. It being Claude though, he took a further two digestifs and coffees to finally announce his answer.

84

'So, let me get this right,' said Peter. 'You are telling me that the builders in France don't see why they should actually look for work, but that it should naturally gravitate towards them because of their reputation. Is that what you are saying?'

Peter was trying to stay calm. He had sat patiently through Didier and Henri's summary of what the meetings with the builders had revealed, even when they divulged that the builders they had met said that they didn't necessarily see the opportunity to earn money by fitting Eastney Intérieurs kitchens as a motivating proposition.

'In a nutshell, yes,' said Didier.

Henri added, 'It's not all bad news Peter, they do think that the idea is good and will work over here, it's just that while they believe in the concept on a general level, they aren't quite sure that it is relevant to them individually.'

'God give me strength,' Peter muttered.

'What you need to understand Pete, is that in France, people would rather be respected, than rich,' said Didier.

'That's nonsense Didier, and you know it,' interrupted Peter, 'what people want is to be respected *and* rich, and that is what our proposition gives them.'

Henri said, 'Pete, you're right, but they want to be *seen* to be respected, but they don't want to be *seen* to be rich, and talking about it is quite uncomfortable for them.'

'So, if I try to unravel this, are we saying that they *do* actually see the value, and they *do* think that they'd like to be a part of it, but that they don't want to say that, or be visibly keen to earn extra money?'

Didier said, 'I think that's about the size of it, Pete.'

'Gentlemen, you are an extremely complicated bunch,' said Peter. The three Frenchmen in the room all had faces that said that they thought it was completely the other way around.

85

With another weekend to consider his options, and now being well into November, Peter had been speaking to Sean and Claude on the phone a few times on the Saturday morning. He needed to make some decisions based on the feedback he had been given by the staff and customers but wasn't sure what they needed to be. One thing he knew for sure though, was that time was ticking on and he still wasn't seeing the energy in the business that he wanted. This was partly on the part of the staff, but more worryingly for him, it was on the part of the customers as well. The three of them agreed to meet up on Monday morning at Lille to make some final decisions.

Peter was quieter than usual at home that weekend, and Kim knew to give him a wide berth when he was like that. Garfield, on the other hand, was over the moon with the slowly drowning business as it meant he got more walks, and they were all much longer than usual.

86

Monday morning, 14th November, and the three musketeers were staring at each other in Claude's office at Lille.

'Well chaps,' declared Peter, 'I've decided on a very technical and strategic plan to navigate our way through these rocky waters.'

'Really?' replied Sean.

'Nah,' answered Peter, 'I'm just going to give everybody everything they've asked for.'

Claude laughed and said, 'How long did it take you to come up with that sophisticated plan?'

Peter said, 'A surprisingly long time unfortunately. The way I see it, we are trying to push water uphill at the moment, and given the difficulty of that task, we may as well make it as easy as we possibly can by removing any barrier that anyone puts in our way.'

Sean said, 'Okay, so what specific things are you going to give them?'

Peter said, 'Well, I'd like you both to create a staff incentive to help the managers win the kitchen incentive, bearing in mind it ends in two weeks' time. I'd also like Henri to arrange some radio advertising and some road-side billboards near every depot. We are going to round up the homeowners and deliver them to the builders so that they don't have to look too hard for the work. On top of that, I want a managers' conference in Monaco at the end of December, where we will present the managers with the incentive money – in cash.'

Sean was excited by this as it gave him some great messages for the troops, but Claude was less enthralled. 'We haven't budgeted for any of this Pete and getting that amount of cash together is not as easy as you'd like it to be.'

'I'm sure it's not Claude, but I need you to find a way,' was Peter's dismissive response.

'One more thing,' said Peter, 'don't tell the staff about the advertising yet. Tell them about the staff incentives and Monaco today, but not the other stuff. If you tell them that there is an advertising campaign coming, they will just sit back and wait for the advertising to arrive. I need them to believe that *they* are the only way we are going to get through this. The advertising will be a nice surprise when it lands.'

'Roger that,' said Sean.

87

With the staff incentive decided, Sean spent the rest of that morning giving the news to the depot teams. It was received well by all, and Sean had a sense that some energy may finally be found to get the huge boulder moving. He relayed his sense of optimism to Peter after he had spoken to the last manager, but Peter's response was a rather sober, 'I hope so, we're running out of options... and time.'

Peter and Sean spent the rest of that day in the depots around Lille. There was a definite improvement in the general atmosphere, and they were both encouraged by the fact that people even seemed to be walking a bit quicker. There were people on the telephones talking to potential customers, and warehouse staff were putting products onto pallets. When Peter asked Pierre, the manager of the Seclin depot, how come there seemed to be more going on today than on previous visits, no mention was made of the staff bonuses. All Pierre had to say about it was, 'It's just starting to come together, with the open day we had, and all the phone calls and visits we've made.'

88

It was like a tap had been turned on. When Sean called Peter with the sales figures that night, they were the first time ever that both had enjoyed the conversation. Every depot had sold something, and five out of the nine had sold kitchens. They were still at very poor gross margins but, as Peter frequently said, *they had to start somewhere.*

Claude joined Peter and Sean for dinner that night. They were walking through Parc Henri Matisse and the ramparts that made up the route between the hotel and the Indian restaurant. Even though it was only mid-November, the Christmas lights were already up around the city and children were running around the park with a sense of festive excitement.

Munching heartily on a bowl of poppadoms, the three were noticeably more animated and talkative than usual, with the waiter, Nicolas, even finding it worthy of note, 'Won the lottery, have we?' he remarked.

'Do you know what?' answered Peter, 'I think we might have!'

During the curry, Claude asked if Peter and Sean thought it was the staff bonuses that had created the day's sales. Peter said, 'Well, it would be a heck of a coincidence if the customers had all started demanding products because of the open days and other efforts, on the exact same day that we announced a staff incentive, wouldn't it?'

Claude said, 'Yes, it's quite unlikely, so what do you think that tells us about the business going forward?'

Peter thought for a while, then said, 'Well, if I'm being cynical, it says that the business doesn't need depot managers, it just needs staff, and me throwing money at them.'

'Yes, that's a conclusion I was drawing as well, but we need managers to keep the business going in the right direction, and within the rules,' said Sean.

Peter said, 'I know, and there's something else niggling away at me if I'm honest. What if the managers and staff were actively sitting on this business all along, just waiting for more money to come their way?'

'Now you *are* being cynical,' insisted Claude, to which Peter just said, 'Mmm, I hope so...'

89

Over the following two weeks, and before the ending of the incentives, there was a definite shift in business momentum. Every depot sold at least one kitchen in that time, and the three prizes for selling kitchens to ten different customers were all claimed. The various forms of advertising that Henri had arranged landed toward the end of November and, whilst the depot teams all said that they liked it, no-one could point to any particular new lead or sale that had come as a result of it.

'More money wasted,' said Sean.

Peter replied, 'Au contraire, it's just the opposite. We've seen the sales go up as soon as the incentives were announced, and no noticeable increase in interest coming from the advertising. I would say it's been money extremely *well spent*.'

Peter and Sean found it notable that the three winners of the cash awards were Ahmet from Turkey, and Carlos and Miguel from Portugal. None of the winners were first generation French people. 'What do you think that tells us?' asked Peter over a beer one night.

Sean replied, 'I think it tells a story of community. When I go into those depots, there are usually Turkish or Portuguese builders there just having a coffee and a chat, and I think it comes down to a sense of trust in their own people.'

'That's great,' observed Peter, 'in that it is what the UK business was built on, people dealing with people they trust. It's just a shame that in a country of 60-odd million people, we've found a way to energise about two per cent of them.'

'Come on Pete,' said Sean, 'to quote your own words on the matter, we *had to start somewhere*, and we have done exactly that, we've finally started.'

'Indeed we have,' said Peter, raising his glass to toast Sean. 'Next stop, Monaco.'

90

Peter loved Formula One. He had been a fan for as long as he could remember, and it was a big part of the reason he had chosen this exclusive enclave as the location for the end of year conference. He loved to walk the circuit and tell anybody within earshot of the incidents and accidents that had happened at each corner over the years. He first caught the bug when his Uncle Paul took him to Brands Hatch to see the British Grand Prix in 1982. He could still remember the smells and noise as if it was yesterday, and he became a lifelong fan of Niki Lauda as a result of seeing him win the race.

He had visited Monaco twice before but had never been to the race. He always felt that it was an event that should be done 'properly', and as that included helicopters, five-star hotels and pit lane access, it was considerably beyond his means. But still he dreamed, one day…

The team arrived at the Hotel de Vitesse and scuttled off in various directions to their rooms. Peter had requested a suite so that he had somewhere to do the cash presentations from. Rather than ask for the sea view that he assumed most people would request, he had asked for a view straight down onto the world-famous hairpin bend and spent the first hour of his stay just staring down at it and taking photographs.

He had managed to convince Sean and Claude that they really wanted to walk the circuit with him, and so they set off, initially around the hairpin and then to the corner by the sea and through the tunnel. It never ceased to amaze Peter how narrow the roads were in relation to the speed of the cars. Peter said, 'I can't imagine racing mopeds around here, let alone 200 mile per hour super-cars.' Sean and Claude couldn't help but agree.

The swimming pool part of the race circuit gets turned into an ice-skating rink over Christmas, with a small market and some places to have a drink or a snack. This provided an opportune time for the three of them to have a pit stop of their own and enjoy a beer overlooking the marina. It was a beautiful day, with the sky still a bright uninterrupted blue, and the sun just starting to descend over the horizon. It was fresh, but not cold.

Sean said, 'Just look at those boats, they must cost hundreds of millions, but they are just there, sat empty. It must be great to be able to afford that luxury.'

Peter couldn't help but find that funny. 'You wouldn't spend that money on a boat even if you had it, you'd rather just keep it in your wardrobe and look at it every day.'

'True,' said Sean.

After a short period of reflection, Claude piped up, 'I wonder how much the mooring fees are.'

Peter replied cheerfully, 'Do you ever get on your *own* nerves?'

Claude replied, 'No, I try to save all of my irritating moments for you Pete.'

91

Suited and booted at 6pm, the three incentive winners arrived at Peter's suite to be greeted by a glass of Champagne and a photographer. Claude had managed to find a way to get the cash and had also found some small briefcases so that the presentation could be a bit more *Hollywood*.

The managers all smiled for the photographs of Peter handing over the cases of cash, but Sean couldn't help noticing that it all looked a bit awkward for them. Peter was smiling broadly and with pride, whereas the managers all looked like they just wanted to get out of there.

With the money handed over and the Champagne bottles empty, they made their way to the restaurant to meet up with the others. Peter had tried his best to get a simple meal organised, but it had proved impossible, so a full five-course extravaganza awaited, with copious amounts of jus, coulis and foam for the culinary elite to feast upon.

After the meal, a small band played for about 90 minutes and took requests. Peter asked for *Comme d'habitude*, partly because it was becoming a bit of a theme for the intrepid trio, and partly because he and Sean could sing *My Way* along to it. A good night was had by all, and the next day was one to look forward to. They were each being picked up on the back of a Harley Davidson and riding up into the hills.

92

It was one of those occasions where he could hear something but couldn't quite make out if it was real or a part of a dream. The longer it went on for though, the more he worked out that it was real and he opened his eyes. The clock said 4.21am, and the noise was that of his hotel room phone.

'Mr Simpson?' enquired a high-pitched voice.

'Yes, what is it?' replied a rather tetchy Peter.

'We have a bit of an issue sir. The local police have just called as they have had to arrest two of your party inside the main casino.'

A still blurry eyed Peter said, 'Who? How? What?'

The high-pitched voice said, 'It's a Monsieur Miguel Silva and Monsieur Carlos Santos. I don't know the full details, but it seems that they lost some money and caused a disturbance inside the casino.'

'Where are they now?' enquired Peter.

'In the cells of the station, I'm afraid,' came the unwelcome reply.

93

'How the bloody hell did you two let that happen?' said an irate Peter to his two generals in his suite, early the next morning.

'They went straight to bed once we got back to the bar last night,' pleaded Sean.

'...or not,' said Claude. 'I've been in touch with the casino and they arrived there at 11.24pm and over the next two hours, managed to lose pretty much all of the cash that you gave them last night. They then got a bit loud, so the security guards asked them to leave, and Carlos decided it would be a good idea to square up to one of them. Then, Miguel joined in and the police were there inside about two minutes to take them away.'

'What happens now?' asked Peter.

'The duty officer starts at 9am this morning, so I will go to the police station and see what I can do,' said Claude.

'Ok, there's nothing else we can do until then, so let's crack on with the Harleys. Will you call me as soon as you've been to the station Claude? I'll get your bike to wait here until you get back and then catch us up.'

'No problem,' said Claude.

Claude went straight to the station after his breakfast and was there at eight thirty. He sat quietly where he was asked to, and then, at 9am precisely, was shown through to the duty officer's desk.

Sergeant Dufort took his time to read the details of the offence, and Claude sat patiently while he did so. The room he was in was small, but with many certificates and commendations proudly displayed on the walls. Claude estimated that the man before him was in his mid-30s, so either he was an extremely well decorated young man, or some of the awards belonged to someone else. He didn't want to irritate the policeman by asking.

Having managed to stay silent while the officer read the file, a feat that Claude thought to himself Peter would be proud of, Sergeant Dufort took a deep breath and said, 'We have two choices here Monsieur Houllier. The first is that we charge your two colleagues with assault, which will mean they will be in court this morning and probably released on bail to appear at a later date,'

'OK,' said Claude, 'and Option Two?'

'Option Two is where they accept an official caution, and you assume responsibility to remove them from the Principality within six hours. If you take that responsibility and they don't leave, it will be you in court as well as them, is that clear?'

Claude confirmed that it was and was shown into the cells where the two offenders were being held.

94

Two more forlorn looking individuals it would be difficult to imagine. They had been kept in separate cells overnight but were allowed to sit together in an interview room to talk with Claude.

'What on earth were you thinking?' asked Claude.

Neither replied immediately, but Carlos eventually said, 'Are they going to let us out?'

Claude explained the choices, and they both chose to take the caution.

'You haven't answered my question, what possessed you to cause a fuss inside a Monaco casino?'

Miguel spoke this time and said, 'We had been drinking with you guys, and we had all the cash we had just been given, so we decided to sneak out for an hour to just play at being rich for a while. We basically blew the lot, and when the heavies asked us to leave, it all got a bit unnecessary really, sorry.'

Claude sighed, and said, 'OK, let's get the paperwork done and get you out of here. You'll have to go straight back to the hotel and pack, you know that, don't you?'

'Yes,' they both muttered, looking at the floor.

Claude called Peter and told him the story, and that he would need to stay with the two managers all the way to the departure gates at Nice Airport.

Peter said, 'Well done Claude, let's catch up later with Sean and Didier to talk it through. Shame about the Harley, I'll see if I can sort something out for you later.'

'No need,' replied Claude, 'I've always preferred having four wheels beneath me if I'm honest.'

95

'They've got to go,' was Peter's opening statement with Sean, Claude and Didier that afternoon.

'It's not as simple as that I'm afraid,' said Didier.

'Nothing in France ever is,' grunted Peter.

'Look Pete, you *can* sack them if you wish, but it will probably be very expensive,' said Didier.

'How come? Surely it's gross misconduct for bringing the company into disrepute,' replied Peter.

'A court is highly likely to take the view that as you had *personally* given them the cash, and *personally* poured the Champagne, that *you* were the cause of the problem,' Didier said, calmly. 'Particularly as you are the president of the business. You have to understand Pete, that the courts here are weighted very heavily in favour of the employee, and the more that the judges can fine a business, the less the government ends up having to pay out in benefits.'

Peter said, 'Define very expensive.'

To which Didier replied, 'I've read of cases similar to this where the compensation paid to the employee was over 300,000 euros, and it can easily take over two years to settle.'

'Well, that's one small mercy, I suppose, at least we will be more profitable when it lands in two years' time.'

Claude meekly said, 'Sorry to be the bearer of bad news again Pete, but under accounting law, I have to get the case assessed by an independent lawyer, and an opinion taken on the likely compensation award. I then need to charge that amount to the P&L straight away.'

'Is there no escape?' asked Peter, with his head in his hands.

'Welcome to France,' smiled Didier.

96

With Christmas behind them, and the Monaco incident now a distant memory, although it still stuck in Peter's throat that he couldn't get rid of the two offenders, they were busy closing the accounts for 2016, and making forecasts for 2017 on their first day back after the break.

Whilst the full year numbers for last year were frankly miserable, the momentum that they finished the year on had been encouraging, and it was this that Peter wanted to make the focal point of his commentary to the executive committee and board in London the following week.

With Claude busy creating scenarios and charts of varying shapes and sizes, Peter and Sean went out into the depots to try to keep the momentum that they had witnessed in December alive. This proved to be a bigger challenge than Peter had hoped. The retail companies had started their advertising campaigns for the winter sale period that was allowed by law, and the managers that Peter and Sean spoke to were all talking things down, as if they didn't need to try again until the sale had ended in the middle of February.

However, before all of that was the small matter of greeting everybody in the business after the New Year. Peter was used to saying hello to everyone when he went into depots; he saw it as the very least he could do. This was normally a straightforward handshake and a simple '*Bonjour, ça va?*' He would make a point of seeking everyone out wherever he went so that everyone felt that the business leader was taking the time to talk to them. Post New Year, however, that small greeting turned into a full-on conversation, with the addition of 'Happy New Year', 'Best Wishes' and an enquiry about what they did during the festive break. This proved to be more time consuming than Peter had bargained for, particular with the more talkative members of the team. The irritation that he was experiencing with this French tradition and courtesy was exacerbated by the fact that all the teams seemed to be more interested in standing around the coffee machine exchanging their stories than they did about kick-starting the business again.

'Where's the energy gone?' asked Peter.

'It's still here Pete, but it looks like it's being funnelled into Christmas stories at the moment,' replied Sean.

'Well, what are you going to do about it? We've got to get that boulder moving all over again now, haven't we?' grumped Peter.

Sean answered, 'Yes, it looks like it, but I think, just for now, we should adopt the French philosophy of *laissez-faire*, just until they've got their polite exchanges out of the way.'

Peter snapped, 'Sean, I don't care if they have a huge *laissez-faire* pie, with lashings of *laissez-faire* cream and a huge *laissez-faire* cherry on the top, so long as they are selling kitchens while they eat it!'

A much calmer Peter, and Sean were in McGuires that evening, exchanging their own stories of the Christmas shutdown. Peter said, 'It was the usual mayhem for us, the girls bought all of their kids up, so there were 12 of us on Christmas Day. I spent most of it trying to find a room that wasn't full of kids fighting, and walking Garfield. He got a *lot* of walks over Christmas; I've now got the fittest dog in Kent. How about you?'

'A tale of two halves for me,' replied Sean. 'I went back to York for Christmas itself, caught up with friends and stuff. I then had Christmas Day with my sister and her family, which was good. I think the real reason my sister invited me though, was so that her kids, who are six and eight, had someone to jump on all afternoon while my sister and brother-in-law slept off lunch in front of the telly. Then, on the 28th, I came back to France, and had New Year's Eve with some friends over here, which was nice.'

Peter said, 'What friends are these then? You've never mentioned any friends.'

'Yes, I have,' said Sean, defensively, 'I told you about the walking group in the village. Well, they had a bit of a get together for New Year in one of their houses and invited me along.'

'Sounds like fun,' said Peter, sarcastically, and he started looking around the bar for someone to serve them a beer.

'It wasn't too bad actually,' said Sean. 'There were about 20 people there, and one of them was Elise, a sister of Jean-Claude, the guy I told you about from the corner shop.'

Peter looked up, with a new-found interest in the story. '...and?'

'And nothing really, we got on fairly well and agreed to go ten-pin bowling this weekend. If I was being cynical, I would say that the lady in the corner shop had been doing a bit of match-making all along when she first invited me out for the walk, but I guess it doesn't really matter.'

'Did you tell her that she'll be expected to pay for it?' laughed Peter.

'I'm not that bad... maybe we'll go 50-50.'

98

'Do you want the good news or the bad news?' was the question Didier asked on the phone the next morning.

Peter replied, 'That sounds ominous, go on.'

'Well, your mate Miguel from Monaco wants to leave,' said Didier.

'Brilliant,' said Peter, 'he is a man of morals after all.'

'Maybe,' said Didier, 'there's just the small matter of the settlement package.'

'What settlement package?' enquired Peter, already getting the sense that he wasn't going to like the answer.

'It's called a *rupture conventionnelle* and is an agreement in French law that allows staff and companies to part company, so long as the company pays,' replied Didier.

'What!?' groaned Peter. 'He wants to leave, when he should have been dismissed for gross misconduct just last month, and he wants me to give him some money? You cannot be serious! Please tell me you're joking.'

'Trust me Pete, this is better than it used to be. It was only in 2008 that this possibility was created. Before that, if somebody wanted to leave, they would just turn up each day and do nothing until you dismissed them. Then, the courts would award eye-watering amounts of money, again, to reduce the money the state had to give them. I know this is a bit of a pain Pete, but it really is the best way forward.'

'How much?' asked a despondent Peter.

'It's all about negotiation, but I suspect we'll end up in the twenty- to thirty-thousand-euro territory,' replied Didier.

'Twenty to thirty thousand euros?' exclaimed Peter, 'and that's on top of the ten grand cash he threw away at the casino. How the bloody hell is a company supposed to make any money over here?'

Didier's silence told Peter all he needed to know.

'Go on then, just get him out of the business – today. Is that clear?'

'Will do,' replied Didier.

99

'Well, that went well,' said Didier with a sense of irony when he put the phone down.

'How did he take it?' asked Claude.

'As you might expect, somewhere between utter disbelief and a desire to kill.'

'He doesn't know how good it is now, compared to the old days,' offered Claude.

'Yes, I told him that, but I don't think he really heard it.'

Claude said, 'I think I'll give Sean a quick ring, I could do without both of them wanting to murder an entire nation.'

Sean was slightly more relaxed about the Miguel payment than Peter was. His main concern was that he was about to lose the manager of his top performing depot and in a business based on relationships, losing the manager could only be a bad thing, especially when a lot of the customers were from his direct network of friends and family. 'Oh well,' said Sean, 'I guess this is just today's shit. There'll be a whole lot of different shit to deal with tomorrow.'

Claude replied thoughtfully, 'René Descartes couldn't have put it better himself.'

100

Armed with his presentation to the board, and a commentary that conspicuously omitted to mention the fact that he was working in a country where it seemed literally impossible to actually make a profit, Peter gave an upbeat story of the last eight weeks of trading of 2016 and the forecasts for 2017, both in terms of sales and profitability. There were no questions during the presentation itself, and Peter had learned to view this as a bad thing, as it usually indicated a lack of interest on the part of the audience.

'Let me be very honest with you,' said Bernard after Peter's talk, 'I can see that you managed to get some traction in the latter part of last year, but it hasn't carried on into this year, has it?'

'No,' admitted Peter, 'but...'

'Peter, you had better get going a bit quicker than this, or you might as well just leave your car keys on the desk right now, and I'll let someone else have a crack at it.' The smile on Bernard's face didn't make Peter feel any better.

Thankfully for Peter, the lunch arrived in the break-out room next door, and Bernard, being hungry, diverted his attention from Peter in favour of a chicken salad wrap. Peter did his best to stay out of everybody's way, eat a very brief lunch and get out of there in double quick time.

Fiona wandered over to Peter during the break and said cheerfully, 'Saved by the bell, eh? Did you remember to leave your keys on the desk?'

'He doesn't frighten me,' said Peter.

'Oh, why?' asked Fiona.

Peter laughed and whispered, 'I came by train!'

101

Sean and Peter were hosting a managers' meeting in Paris during the April of 2017. The sales had picked up again after the January lull, Peter had somehow managed to keep hold of his car keys, and Claude was still moaning that the margins were too low.

During a break in the meeting, Sean went out to the car park and caught several managers smoking and admiring his new company car, a BMW 5 series. He said, 'Nice isn't it, I only picked it up last week.'

Pierre, the manager from the Seclin depot, said, 'It's beautiful, what is it like to drive?'

Sean answered, 'Like a dream, Pierre.'

Pierre stared longingly at the car and just said, 'Amazing.'

Sean told Peter of this conversation when he went back into the meeting room, and Peter said, 'Maybe we can use this to our advantage.'

With the meeting finished, the group made their way to Head Office, McGuires, for an aperitif before a plate of Suri's finest. At the pub, Peter engineered a conversation that resulted in Sean talking about his new car, and Peter said to the team, 'I'll tell you what, why don't I rent a 5 series BMW for a year, and award it each month to the top performing depot manager as recognition of a good month's sales?'

In a similar response to when he had offered the cash incentives, the table fell quiet. Sean, convinced that at least one of the managers would find this a motivating offer, said to Pierre, 'So then Pierre, do you think you've got what it takes to win it?'

Pierre replied, rather meekly, 'It is a fine car.'

On the walk between McGuires and Suri's, Peter said to Sean, 'Do you think I'm wasting money with the car incentive?'

Sean replied, 'No, I just think that they don't want to be seen to be too keen. At the very least, it can't do any harm, can it.'

'I suppose not,' said a mystified Peter.

Henri had asked if there could be a product review, because with six months' sales under their belts, they could now make some informed decisions about the selection they had started with.

'Do you want me to generate some margin related numbers on the product sales, Claude?' asked Henri.

'Not really, thanks. I've got all the numbers if we need them, but he never listens to a word I say about margin. It's just sales, sales, sales with him.'

Henri said, 'I know what you mean, I've sold some of these products for decades, and I've never seen margins this low before, but when I mention it, he just says that there's no point addressing margin until we are selling enough product to at least break even.'

Claude sighed, 'Yes, same here, but if we had higher margins, we could be breaking even already. I'll try again in the product meeting, but I don't hold out much hope.'

'I bet Henri bangs on about us not selling any blinds,' said Sean, as he was driving to Lille with Peter for the product meeting.

'Have we sold any at all?' asked Peter.

'Not to my knowledge. I've seen mailshots and posters in the depots advertising them, but I don't know of any sales.'

Peter said, 'Well, fair enough, we gave it a go.'

Pleasantries exchanged, and coffee sourced, the four of them sat down with the packs that Henri had created. These were not insignificant packs and looked like Claude had been a large part of the creation process. 'Shall we start at the beginning then Pete?' asked Henri.

'Actually, no Henri, could you please start at the end, which is where I assume your recommendations are, and if there are any that I want to challenge, we can go and look at the data on just those.'

Henri, slightly deflated by having his two hours of glory snatched from him, read the list of products that he believed they should discontinue. Blinds were top of the list, followed by four kitchen ranges, some flooring, and a few bits of hardware. Peter looked at Sean and said, 'Is that OK with you?'

Sean nodded, and Peter said, 'Good, that's decided then. Now, do you have any recommendations of products we wish to introduce?'

Claude couldn't pipe up quick enough, 'More? Pete, we've got warehouses full of the stock we've just discontinued. Can't we get rid of that first?'

Peter looked at him, and said, 'Claude, we need the products that the customers want to buy from us *today*, not in three years' time when we've finally got rid of all the blinds that some idiot insisted on stocking.'

Henri read a list of some of the things that the managers had asked him for, and Sean added a few appliances that he had heard requests for. The whole meeting was done before their first coffee was cold, and Peter said, 'That was great guys, thanks very much.'

As he got out of his chair to leave the meeting, Claude said, 'Can we please talk about gross margins Pete?'

Peter sat down again and replied, 'Claude, working with you is like working with toothache.'

Claude smiled and said, 'I'll take that as a compliment.'

A 30-minute summary of where they were haemorrhaging margin followed, which Peter sat politely through. When finished, Claude sat back in the belief that he had at least made some impact.

Peter said, 'How does our margin compare to the UK business?'

Claude replied, 'About half as good.'

Peter said, 'OK, that means it's probably still a bit high.'

Claude stared in amazement, so Peter said, 'Look Claude, and you Henri, I need you to both understand what's going on out there. The depot teams think that they are fighting on price, but they're not. What they are doing is fundamentally changing how a market currently functions, and that's tough. They are convincing builders to get involved in buying kitchens, and about how our entire offering is geared up to encouraging and helping them. Price is just one element, but the credit terms, design service, and most of all stock, are huge advantages we have. Once we have a critical mass of builders that buy into the concept, they will pay the correct price for the products. Until we have that critical mass, we don't really have a business worth investing in. We need to do this job in the right order, and margin is not my primary concern right now. I'm much more interested in how many new customers we've signed up and how many new designs we've created. There will be a time for margin increase, and it won't be easy, but that time is not yet. Does that make sense? Because I need us all to be on the same page on this one.'

Claude and Henri both nodded, and Henri said, 'It's quite impressive what they've done already really in terms of volumes.'

Peter said, 'Yes it is, and the job for Sean and I is to keep the momentum and energy going so that we hit that critical mass and, sometimes, that feels like walking through a swamp full of treacle with lead boots on, but we have to keep on fighting.'

103

Before long, it was May again. The roads were quiet and the depots were empty. Sean decided to go into one of the Lille depots, the one at Englos. The car park had one solitary car in it, that belonging to Louis, the manager, and when he walked in, Louis was sitting alone in the back office.

'Hi Louis, how are you today?' enquired Sean cheerfully.

'Up to my neck in it, if I'm honest Sean,' came the rather stressed reply.

'Oh, sorry to hear that,' said Sean. 'Where is everyone?'

Louis replied, 'I'm on my own until 11am when my designer will arrive. Everybody else is either on holiday or using up lieu days.'

Sean was helping Louis with his latest customer promotion and the designer had finally shown her face when his phone rang. It was Paul Barratt, the head of the UK audit team. 'Hi Sean, how's it going?' asked Paul.

'Good thanks Paul, how can I help?'

Paul said, 'I'm afraid I have some bad news. We've just conducted a stock audit at Massy depot in Paris, and the result is an enormous loss. I'll email you the details, but it's one of the worst I've ever seen.'

'Ouch,' said Sean. 'What happens now?'

Paul said, 'Well, for my part, I have to report it to the board, and go back to that depot in six months' time. It's your call regarding any disciplinary action you take, but in my experience of the UK depots, they would replace at least the manager if there had been that level of loss, but that is very much your department. I'll need to know what you do though, as a part of my board report.'

Sean said, 'OK Paul, thanks for that, I think. I'll let you know what happens.'

104

'How much?' said a shocked Peter when Sean called him with the news.

Sean whispered the number as quietly as he could, as if it somehow made the news more palatable.

'Bloody hell, Sean, that's about a quarter of his entire stock holding. How the hell do you lose that much gear without noticing? You'd need an articulated lorry to move that much stock!'

'I know, I'm going there now, and I'll call Didier about how to play it,' said Sean.

The dejection in Sean's voice was clear, so Peter cheerfully said, 'Fancy a curry tonight?'

Sean replied, 'Yes, I think I could do with it.'

'OK, 6.30pm at Head Office for a beer then,' said Peter.

Peter was already pondering a different problem before Sean called him about the stock loss.

Claude had called him over the weekend while he was doing some shopping and said that he thought that they might need to get rid of Gabrielle Dubois, the credit control manager. He'd had a call from Fiona about the success of debt collection in France compared to the UK, and it wasn't good news. The level of debt that the French business was writing off was such that it would make the whole business unsustainable if it didn't improve significantly. When Claude had looked into the individual case files of the debt write-offs, it was clear to him that the customers concerned should never have been given credit in the first place.

After a few seconds to reflect, Peter said, 'OK, let's think on over the weekend, and speak again on Monday.'

Peter called Claude back after he had spoken to Sean about the stock loss and said, 'I'm not sure that getting rid of Gabrielle is the right thing to do, not at this stage anyway.'

Claude replied, '...but Fiona said that it might be best all round if we changed horses sooner, rather than later.'

Peter said, 'That's easy for her to say, but at the end of the day, it's not her that's got to collect the debt, it's us.'

'So what do you think we should do?' asked Claude.

'Well, the big issue here is not the financial write off, it's about ownership. If there's a huge chunk of potential write off that we can see, there's likely to be treble that in debt that is still sitting in the ledger waiting to become overdue, isn't there?' said Peter.

Claude said, 'I guess so.'

Peter continued, 'So, if we get rid of Gabrielle and appoint a new head of credit control, he or she will take the viewpoint that everything currently in the ledger is uncollectable, as they will want a clean sheet for themselves. Nobody will "own" the current debt, and that could be a very serious issue for us.'

Claude said, 'Sorry Pete, I feel I've let the side down here. I should have had better controls in place.'

Peter laughed and said, 'Claude, don't worry about it. Do you fancy a curry in Paris tonight?'

Peter decided he should let Bernard know of the issues he was dealing with, so he picked a time that he was fairly sure the call would go straight to the messaging service and called him. Unfortunately for him, Bernard picked it straight up, and whereas Peter had mentally prepared the message he was going to leave, he wasn't prepared to speak to the man himself.

'How's it going Peter?' asked Bernard.

'Well, that was why I called actually, we are having a few problems with stock losses and debt collection at the moment, but we're on the case with it.'

'Yes, I'd heard about both from over here, so I was expecting your call.'

'To be honest Bernard, I think that there will be debt issues and stock losses coming down the line for a few months now, as the fixes I can put in place today won't affect the damage that's already in the system, as it were.'

Bernard replied, 'Okay, it sounds like you've done as much as you can for now. Keep digging.'

105

'It's OK for you two, it's me that had to poke the bear this afternoon with all of our good news,' said Peter, smiling broadly when they met in McGuires that evening.

'How was he?' asked Sean.

'He was fine actually, he just said that we need to understand how we've arrived here, and make sure that it doesn't happen again, and that, gentlemen, is exactly what we are going to do.'

Over their aperitifs, they formed a plan. Sean was going to go through all the items that the depot at Massy had 'mislaid' to see if he could make any connections. If it was complete kitchens, he might be able to identify which ones they were. Claude was going to help Gabrielle get on top of the debt ledger by recruiting some short-term assistance to help with the current debt. He was also going to look at the files that weren't yet overdue and might benefit from some early efforts at collection. Claude himself was going to review each file with Gabrielle and decide on a priority action list.

All being content with the actions they had agreed, the general mood around the table lifted, such that by the time they were looking down at France's finest food in Suri's, they were back ribbing Claude about the fact that the only other contender so far for 'Best food in France' wasn't actually in France at all.

'So, Sean, how are you getting on with Elise then?' asked Claude, while wiping a considerable amount of spilled Madras sauce off his shirt.

'Yes, Mr Bond, you don't talk about her very much,' added Peter.

'I could say the same about you two,' said a slightly defensive Sean. 'It's fine, we see each other most weekends, she has her place in the village, and I have mine within walking distance, so it works out well really. Neither of us are after anything heavy, so we just go with the flow. It's good.'

Claude launched into a monologue about how, sometimes, two peoples' perceptions of the same relationship can be very different, until Peter interjected, 'Why don't you just eat your curry – at least the bit that you aren't wearing, and let the poor man live his own life.'

Claude looked down at his shirt and said, 'I guess it is difficult to take me seriously at the moment.'

Sean continued eating his meal and muttered, '...*at the moment?*' to which Claude replied indignantly, 'I heard that!'

On the way back to the hotel after the curry, Peter asked if the others fancied a nightcap. Sean nodded, but Claude said that he wasn't staying, as it was the Bank Holiday the next day, so he was getting the TGV back to Lille. They both waved him off and Sean called out, 'Don't nod off and wake up in Brussels.'

Claude called back, 'It wouldn't be the first time I've done that!'

Peter shouted, 'If you do end up in Belgium, could you bring us some decent food back?'

Claude didn't grace the comment with a response.

106

Having dealt with pages of unread emails, largely by deleting them ('If it's really important, they'll write again,' were Peter's words to himself as he pressed the magic button), he decided to have a drive around the industrial zones where they had depots to see if there was any life in any of them on a Bank Holiday.

It was a mixed bag. They had chosen some buildings on heavy industrial estates, and they were absolutely dead. On the mixed-use estates though, it was a slightly different story, with the retail occupants open on the holiday and trading as normal. This was bringing traffic to the areas near Eastney Intérieurs' depots to the point where Peter wondered if it might be useful opening a couple of depots as a test to see what happened.

It was on one of those types of estates, in Nanterre, that Peter was nearly at their depot. Nanterre was proving itself to be a consistently good performer, and Peter was wondering if it was a sign that the location requirements in France might be different to the UK.

As he arrived at the depot, he could see the incentive car parked outside, the BMW 5 series. It was extremely dirty, and Peter assumed that Ahmet, the manager, was working that day for some reason. He tried the door, but it was locked, and a walk around the perimeter indicated that no-one was present.

He called Sean and, after apologising for calling on a Bank Holiday, asked if he knew why the car might be parked at the depot. Sean said, 'No idea, I'll give him a ring.'

Ten minutes later, Sean called back and said, 'Are you sitting down?'

'He said that he doesn't want to take the car home, as his neighbours would see it and he doesn't want them to think that he's come into some money or is being ostentatious.'

Peter said, 'Wow, that's bizarre. If it was me, I'd be driving up and down the street honking my horn just so the neighbours *did* see it.'

Sean said, 'Me too, maybe it wasn't such a good idea after all. He said that if he was being honest, he would prefer however much we are paying per month to rent it, as extra bonus.'

Peter said, 'That's crazy. OK, I will add that to the list of things that I don't understand about the French.'

Sean laughed and said, 'How long is that list now, Pete?'

He laughed back and said, 'It is starting to turn into a very weighty tome indeed.'

107

It took Sean about two weeks to do the full investigation into the stock loss at Massy. Whether it was his deep-rooted love of conspiracy theories making him suspect everything and everyone, or just a burning urge to get the job done, he didn't know, but he quite enjoyed it and devoted every waking moment to getting to the bottom of it. He spent a fair amount of his sleeping ones devoted to it as well.

'I think we've got a systems issue Pete,' was Sean's opening comment to Peter on the phone.

'OK, how so?' asked Peter.

'I think something happened when we were doing all the adaptations,' said Sean, 'because the UK system is fine, but what's been happening here is that when they turn an estimate into an invoice, it's been knocking off random products. The issue is, though, that the products are still on the picking list that goes out to the warehouse staff, so the kitchens have been going out in full, but on many occasions, certain products aren't on the invoice. It's not any particular products, or customers, it is completely random. It's never thousands of euros on any one invoice either, it's a plinth here, a panel there or the odd unit, so it didn't get picked up as a matter of course.'

'Shit Sean, does that mean we've got loads more bad audits coming down the line?'

'Don't know yet, I've been speaking to Yasmine and she's looking into it.'

108

Over the summer months of 2017, customer numbers grew, sales grew, even the margin grew, but only very slightly, and not nearly enough to make Claude happy. The debt collection rate improved, largely due to Claude almost running the department himself while Gabrielle tightened up on her own credit checks. The policy of chasing up future debt even before it was due had a positive effect, and a more aggressive attitude to older outstanding debt also proved fruitful. It still wasn't as good as the UK business, but the marked improvement gave hope to the likes of Fiona, who was an important person to keep onside.

The stock loss issue was reasonably quickly fixed once identified. The damage was done though in all the other depots, and stock losses were experienced almost everywhere, some of them quite significant. The problem was indeed caused during the adaptations, as Sean had guessed. However, all attempts to apportion responsibility to the software company proved futile. The blame seemed to lie everywhere and nowhere, with lawyers burning the midnight oil scrutinizing contracts. In the end, Peter decided it wasn't worth the distraction and put it behind him. August came and went, with the usual exodus to the south coast, and the BMW 5 series remained largely unused.

With a considerably bigger business than at the same time the previous year, Peter assumed that the October sales period would be a little easier. The issue for him this year though, was how to get a business that comes to a grinding halt in August, back to full throttle by October – just four short weeks away.

Peter, Sean and Claude had spent many days and evenings during the summer discussing how this might happen, and between them had decided that an incentive on new kitchen designs created for customers in September might help kitchen sales in October, so Sean had arranged a managers' meeting for the first week in September, when they were all back from holiday.

Peter was on the A1, driving down from Lille to Paris to attend the meeting that Sean had arranged. He was driving as quickly as he could, but there were more and more speed cameras on the A1 appearing. It used to be the case that there was but one, and conveniently placed at the 130km mark from Paris. He assumed it was a gentle reminder of the speed limit that everyone should be adhering to. As he was approaching the toll station just north of Paris, Sean called. 'Hi Pete, bit of a problem I'm afraid, I've been involved in an accident on the *périphérique*.'

Peter said, 'Sorry to hear that, everyone OK?'

Sean replied, 'Yes, just car damage, but I can't get to the meeting tonight now, shall I cancel it?'

Peter said, 'No, that's fine, I'll do it on my own.' As they were both about to hang up, Peter laughed and said, 'Oh, Sean, by the way, I know where there's a 5 Series going spare.'

The meeting room was particularly relaxed when Peter arrived, with all of the newly bronzed managers discussing their various summer antics and laughing together. He was already getting a bad feeling about this meeting, which was confirmed when it took him three attempts to get everyone seated and paying attention. He noted that they all found time to grab a coffee before they sat down though.

After he had revealed the incentives and talked about the objectives for October, there were no comments or questions from the audience. When he pushed a bit harder, Thomas from Massy said, 'We will do our best Pete, but it's *la rentrée* at the moment, so the customers aren't really thinking about work yet.'

Peter said, 'Excuse me? The whole country has been closed for a month; it's time to get going again now. What is this *la rentrée* thing anyway?'

Carlos from Pantin depot said, 'It's this time of year when everyone goes back to school or work and are just getting back into the swing of things.'

Peter said, 'So let me get this right. In France you've actually got a word for the time of year when you are back at work, but don't actually feel the need to *do* anything?'

Carlos said, 'Well, I wouldn't put it quite like that myself, but basically… yes.'

109

When Peter told Sean about the previous night's meeting and the bizarre concept of working, but not working, he wasn't surprised. He said, 'Yes, I had the same issue when I was teaching over here, it's almost impossible to get them moving again after the holidays until they feel they've had their re-entry time.'

Peter said, 'Well, we need to buck the trend, so can we push harder for sales than we normally would please, so that they get the message that the holidays are most certainly over.'

Sean said, 'Of course,' to placate him, when actually he knew that it didn't matter what he did; it would just take the time that it naturally does in France.

Sean's first depot visit that day was the one at Meaux, to the east of Paris. It was managed by Efe, another of the Turkish contingent and an old friend of Ahmet from Nanterre. When he got there, there was a lady that Sean didn't recognise in the back office looking through some papers. He introduced himself to the visitor, and she announced herself as Madame Allard, a government appointed bailiff. Sean sounded concerned by this news, but Madame Allard quickly put his mind at ease by saying that she was purely there to oversee some products being disposed of. With Sean's pulse rate starting to normalise, he went through to Efe's office and grabbed himself a coffee.

'So how long has she been here then?' asked Sean.

Efe said, 'About 30 minutes I suppose. She made a call when she got here, then I showed her the pallets of damaged stock and the documentation, and she stamped and signed our paperwork. She's been on her laptop for the last ten minutes or so.'

Sean said, 'So how does she know that the products on the paperwork tie up with the products on the pallets? Did you have to identify every piece?'

Efe said, 'No, she just had a quick look around the pallets and that was that.'

'So, what is the point of her coming here then, if she doesn't understand our product range?' asked Sean.

Efe gave a deep shrug of the shoulders and said, 'It keeps someone in work, I suppose.'

Sean asked, 'How much do we pay for this privilege?'

Efe said, '200 euros.'

Sean shook his head and said, 'I'm in the wrong bloody job.'

110

Peter was happily listening to Nostalgi, a French radio station that specialised in French and British oldies, while he was driving up the A1 to Lille from Paris. The road was so straight and boring that Peter was sure he could just wedge the steering wheel in place and have a two-hour nap sometimes. Midway through *Bat out of Hell* by Meatloaf, Didier called. 'Hi Pete, are you heading anywhere near the office in the next few days please?'

Peter replied, 'I'll be there in about an hour, is that quick enough?'

Didier said, 'Perfect. We need to set up a workers' council soon. I've been batting it away as long as possible, but the time has come, I'm afraid.'

Peter said, 'Is it problematic?'

To which Didier's response was, 'Not really, not with a company our size. It's just a few more French hoops to jump through, and another shelf full of paperwork that no-one ever looks at.'

Didier had already prepared the paperwork that Peter needed to sign by the time he got to Lille. Peter said, 'So, what's involved in having a workers' council then?'

Didier said, 'Well, the idea is that workers are consulted about any issues concerning the business as a whole, like restructurings, major redundancies, that sort of thing. It's supposed to give the staff a voice at the top table.'

Peter said, '...and in reality?'

Didier answered, 'In reality, it's a lot of bureaucracy and paperwork for us, and in my experience, the only people that apply to be elected onto it are those that want a bit of time out of the office once a month to attend the meetings, or people that – shall we say – underperform, and view it as a way of keeping their job. It is almost impossible to get rid of someone that's on the workers' council.'

Peter laughed and said, 'Do employers get *any* rights in France Didier?'

Didier smiled and said, 'Oh definitely, they have the right to pay wages and taxes – but not necessarily in that order!'

'To what extent do I have to do what they want?' asked Peter.

'It's more about consultation than having any rights to request anything,' answered Didier. 'They *can* ask for things, but if you don't want to do it, you just say no. It's the same with the consultation, if you want to do something and they say no, you can still do it, you just have to document the fact that they disagreed.'

Peter was astounded by this. 'So, what's the point of the workers' council in the first place then?'

Didier said, 'Well, apart from the reasons I've already given you, it's just a part of living in France really. The employer is always viewed as the bad guy, and the government is there to protect the workers against corporate tyrants. That's you, by the way,' Didier said, with his most Cheshire Cat-like grin.

Peter ignored the comment and said, 'Do I have to go to all these meetings personally?'

Didier said, 'No, you can delegate the responsibility to me, if you wish.'

Peter returned the cat-like grin and said, 'Consider it delegated.'

111

The October sale period went well. Peter and Sean weren't sure how, if they were honest. Peter said to Sean that it was a bit like when he used to go to a depot while they were being fitted out. You never actually saw any work in progress, but somehow, it always got completed on time. Peter had said that it was as if they chose to drink coffee and smoke all day, and then turn into their alter-egos of relentless workaholics during the dark hours. Sean laughed and said, 'Relentless workaholics? I'll remind you of that, one day.'

There was never a huge increase in visible energy in the depots when the *rentrée* period ended, although it had no defining end date that Peter and Sean could identify. Things just moved along at their usual, lethargic pace throughout September and then into October. Nothing seemed particularly urgent in the depots, but when the sales figures came through at the end of each day, they were pleasantly surprised.

The result of the October trading period was that all nine depots had record sales figures, and so Peter wanted to mark that achievement with a good end-of-year event. After the previous year's debacle in Monaco, however, he was going to take a bit of time to decide on the location. Claude said that the south of France was still a good bet, but that they could maybe look for a hotel that was a bit more remote, so that no-one could escape like they did previously. Peter asked Claude to look into it and come back with some suggestions.

112

'Idiot,' was Fleur's initial response when Claude told her that he had suggested somewhere for the conference and had now been tasked with finding a hotel. She was well aware of the mess that they had all got into in Monaco and how Claude had spent much of his time negotiating with heavily armed police to secure the release of their wayward managers. 'You do realise who's going to get the blame for anything that goes wrong at this one, don't you?'

Claude just stared at his laptop, searching through website after website and said, 'Why would anything go wrong at this one?'

Fleur started reading a newspaper and quietly re-iterated, 'Idiot.'

After about three hours of research and a couple of glasses of particularly pleasant Burgundy, Claude announced, 'This is tough; tougher than I thought.'

Fleur just looked at him, and he continued, 'Everything that's suitable seems to be shut in December, and the few that aren't are all using the time to do major works while they stay open.'

Fleur said, 'Show me the options.'

Claude showed her the three that were possible, in that they were remote, and weren't warning potential customers of their stay being disrupted by pneumatic drills.

'Is that it? Three hotels in the whole of the south of France?' said Fleur.

Claude answered, 'Well, it needs to be a coach ride from an airport or train station really, and not more than an hour if possible.'

Fleur glanced at the three websites, and said, 'That one.'

Claude said, 'Perfect,' to which Fleur replied, 'Why is it perfect?'

Claude answered, 'Because you chose it, and not me.'

113

Sean was using the time between the end of the sale period and Christmas to decide what he wanted to do over the festive period and, more importantly, where he wanted to spend it. He had been spending a lot of time with Elise at the weekends, and she had invited him to hers for Christmas Day lunch along with her parents and brother. Whilst this was convenient, it all sounded a bit too much like *happy families* for Sean. His other option was to go back to York, where the day itself would be another time of being jumped on by nieces and nephews, but he would get a few good nights out in York with his friends to offset it. On balance, he decided to go to York and told Elise while they were in a restaurant one Saturday night in mid-November. 'Oh, OK,' said Elise, 'I hope you have fun.'

It didn't take a degree in psychology for Sean to work out that he had just given the wrong answer. Sean changed the subject shortly after that, but the tone of the evening swiftly descended into being more around polite exchanges than it was around conversation. When Elise told Sean at the end of the meal that she wasn't feeling too well and would be going home instead of staying at Sean's that night, he started to wonder if he'd made the right decision about Christmas. Or about Elise.

114

'Try to stay out of jail,' were Kim's wise words for the day while Peter was packing to go to the December conference.

'It wasn't me in jail, as you very well know,' declared Peter, indignantly.

'Should have been,' said Kim, only half joking. 'Fancy giving people thousands of euros of cash, in Monaco. What exactly did you *think* would happen?'

Peter said, 'We've all moved on from that, thank you. Well, most of us have anyway.'

With a parting kiss, Peter headed off to Lydd Airfield, about a 40-minute drive away. He had managed to get a good price from Frank Baines to fly him straight to Nice and back, so was looking forward to flying without any of the fuss and bother of going through a large airport. At Lydd, he would be in the air 15 minutes after he locked his car – or at least that was the plan. During the drive to Lydd, the phone rang and Peter could see that it was Frank calling. 'Hello Frank, I'll be there in 20,' Peter cheerfully declared.

Frank replied, 'I've got a bit of a problem Pete. Bernard's just called me and wants me in Dundee this morning, so I'm just off there now.'

Peter said, 'So where does that leave me?'

Frank replied, 'I will still get you to Nice, but I'm going to have to arrange another plane for you now, so you'll have to wait at the airport until it arrives. I'll give you a ring when I know when that will be.'

It was 50 minutes before Frank called Peter back, and a further one hour and 40 minutes until the replacement aircraft arrived. As the officials at Lydd were only recently aware of the change, there were further delays while the airport staff followed their protocols. It was almost three hours after his planned departure time that Peter finally took off in his flying cigar tube. The irony of the fact that he would have already been there if he had chosen to fly commercially, and at a fraction of the price, was not lost on Peter, as he took off and was almost immediately looking down at the English Channel beneath him.

115

The hotel that Claude had booked was on a vast estate that encompassed a vineyard and a full 18-hole golf course, much to the delight of Claude and a few others. The floors and rooves of the buildings on the estate were clad in terracotta tiles, and the external walls were all painted white. It was a look that Peter had noticed was very common as he took his taxi from Nice Airport to the Bandol region where the hotel was, an hour's drive.

Even with his delay, he was still the first of the group to arrive, with everyone else due to arrive at about 4pm, so he took full advantage of the situation and used the hotel's spa facilities.

Fully invigorated after his leisure time, Peter went down to meet the two coaches when they arrived, one from Nice Airport and the other from Marseilles train station. Even though it was December, the climate was pleasant and it was still bright daylight at 4pm. The hotel staff were all still wearing shorts and short sleeved shirts, an indication of a weather system somewhat different to the one in the north of France that they were arriving from. With no disaster stories to tell from either coach, everyone checked in to the hotel and agreed to meet in the hotel bar at 6.30pm. Even without any reportable incidents, Peter noticed that some of the party from the train looked more animated than normal and wondered if they had inadvertently stumbled into the buffet carriage en-route.

Dinner was as plain as Peter was able to specify, but it still came with swirls of different coloured sauces and mounds of foam, distracting the diner from what was – in Peter's opinion at least – a pretty average piece of beef. The wine was exceptional though. It was from the hotel's own estate, and much to the horror of the waiting staff, Peter insisted on there being bottles of wine placed on the table so that the party could help themselves. Peter explained that the hotel would probably sell more wine this way, but it was an argument that fell on deaf ears as far as the head waiter was concerned. Peter was sure he heard him mutter *'putain!'* as he walked from the table, but didn't make an issue of it.

With dinner out of the way, the group retired to the bar. Peter made his excuses and went to his room, and Sean and Claude were given strict instructions to make sure no-one escaped this time around. Claude said, 'Pete, we are ten kilometres away from any form of civilization, they can't escape this time.'

Peter smiled and said, 'Famous last words!'

Determined that no incidents or accidents were going to blight this year's conference, Claude and Sean made a point of staying up until the bitter end, making a mental note of everybody that left to go to bed and satisfying themselves that nobody was looking as if they had some ulterior motive as they left the bar area. It was approaching 3am when the two of them were finally able to sign off the bar bill and make their way up to their rooms. The hour was such that the cleaners were mopping the reception floor, thus rendering the lifts unavailable, so they decided to use the ornate and expansive staircase; it being their token gesture at exercise for that day.

As they approached the third floor, they could hear some mumbling and laughing. Sean tugged gently at Claude's shirt and put his finger to his mouth to urge a quiet approach. It sounded like Pierre from Seclin depot and Efe from Meaux depot, and they appeared to be outside the lift on the third floor.

'...about three thousand,' said Pierre. 'And you?'

'Only two for me,' replied Efe.

'It was a shame that the stock audits came along and highlighted it really,' added Efe.

'Yes, we could have been making money for years because of their wonderful IT system,' laughed Pierre quietly.

'Oh well, good night,' said Efe.

Pierre was in the middle of returning the exchange when they were both faced with Sean and Claude, who swiftly appeared in front of them. The startled look of both told a story in itself, and

Sean was quick to capitalise on the element of surprise. 'So, just two thousand for you then Efe?'

Both Efe and Pierre looked down at the floor and started to blush. Claude couldn't help himself and had to fill the ensuing silence with words. 'How could you? This company has been nothing but fantastic to the pair of you, and this is how you repay that!'

Neither of the managers spoke, so Sean said, 'I suggest we talk about this in the morning.'

He and Claude then walked back downstairs and left the managers to think about their actions overnight.

116

Sean held on until 6am before he picked the phone up and dialled Peter. He hadn't bothered going to bed himself, not that he was feeling tired. Angry, betrayed and disappointed – yes, but not tired. He filled Peter in on the events by the lift and waited for a response.

'Shit. How widespread to you think it is? asked Peter.

'Difficult to say at the moment, but I've been thinking about that myself,' replied Sean.

'Have you spoken to Didier about it?' enquired Peter.

'No, not yet,' answered Sean.

'OK, we need to do that, so I suggest you tell the two of them to stay in their rooms until we say otherwise, and I'll give Didier a call.'

Sean, Claude, Didier and Peter had a breakfast meeting on the balcony of Peter's room. The stunning views of the seemingly endless vineyards being washed in the beautiful morning sunlight gave a setting that appeared like one of celebration, and Peter felt almost guilty having to tarnish such a backdrop with the grim subject matter in hand. 'Where do we stand then Didier?' was Peter's first question.

'Could go one of two ways Pete,' answered Didier. 'We need to interview them properly, and we can't do that here and now, as they have the right to legal or union representation if they wish. If, during the interview, they admit theft, we can dismiss them and report it to the police. If they don't, however, we are on a stickier footing, as our own investigations at the time didn't highlight an issue. The fact that they've now had all night to get their stories aligned doesn't help matters either.'

Peter said, 'So, assuming that they don't admit it, where does that leave us?'

Didier said, 'You're not going to like this Pete, but if they come up with an even moderately reasonable explanation for the conversation that Sean and Claude overheard, then we can't do much at all really.'

Peter said, 'If you're going to tell me that we are going to have to pay these two to leave, like we did the last ones, then just don't.'

Didier looked at Peter and said, 'If my experience is anything to go by, that is the most likely outcome if they don't admit anything fraudulent.'

Peter shook his head in disgust at this news while staring blankly at the horizon, but suddenly the view from his balcony had lost its shine.

Didier said, 'I will talk to them both, send them home, and tell them that we will be interviewing them formally in due course.'

Peter said, 'What is today's activity Claude?'

He replied, 'Go-karting at Paul Ricard racing circuit. The bus leaves at 10am.'

Peter said, 'OK, can you skip that please Didier. Wait until we've all gone and then talk to them both. Can you make sure that they are both out of the way by the time we get back please? I don't want to set eyes on either of them.'

Didier said, 'No problem. I'm not really built for go-karting anyway!'

Peter laughed politely, and then looked at Sean and said, 'We could have a huge issue here. They could *all* be on the make.'

117

The rest of the conference was a low-key affair. The day at the race track was fun, but there was a definite air of uncertainty about it. Sean and Peter assumed that the other managers knew of the situation, if only because two of their number were missing and nobody asked why. Peter and Sean, for their part, couldn't help but have half a mind on the fact that they could currently be spending time among a syndicate of organised criminals. It was as much as they could do to smile politely and get through the whole thing as quickly as possible.

118

Didier was able to arrange the interviews with Pierre and Efe for the week following the conference, which was also the week before the Christmas shutdown. Neither chose to have representation, and neither admitted any wrongdoing. They both came up with a similar story about them referring to sums of bonus they had earned. When Didier pushed them on the comment about the *wonderful IT system*, they both said that it was an entirely unconnected statement. They both also said that they would like to leave the company if the *arrangements* were acceptable.

When Didier told Sean and Peter about the conversations, it didn't trigger the verbal explosion he was expecting. They had both had time to reflect on the consequences of each outcome, and the two interviewees admitting theft and implicating every other manager at the same time, was by far the most damaging. Even the fact that they now had to pay to get rid of them didn't hit the raw nerve that Didier assumed it would.

Peter said, 'If it costs us ten grand or so to get rid of them, and we haven't got to dismiss every other manager in the business, then I guess it's as good an outcome as we could hope for… Christ, what am I saying?'

119

The Christmas shutdown in 2017 couldn't come quickly enough for Peter. The fact that he had to pay two people that he considered to be thieves to leave the business left a taste in his mouth that he didn't think any amount of Christmas Day Champagne was going to take away.

As was usual for Peter, he didn't share too many of the grisly details that were bothering him at home while he was on his Christmas break. He saved that particular privilege for his long walks with Garfield, who provided his usual ways of dealing with such matters, one of which was to find as many muddy puddles as he could and run through them in a figure-of-eight manner until he was wearing all of the mud that had previously lie dormant. Peter smiled when he concluded that what he was watching Garfield do was a reasonable metaphor for his own life working in France.

During the week or so that Peter had off, he managed to compartmentalise the different issues he was dealing with. There was little to be gained by viewing everybody as criminals unless or until facts emerged to suggest otherwise. Further, it was up to him to keep the energy levels high for the whole of the business, as poorly motivated salespeople are never successful salespeople.

So, refreshed and recharged, Peter returned to France in the January of 2018, determined that this was the year that they were going to turn the corner and become an attractive investment for expansion.

...or crash and burn.

PART THREE

SCALABILITY

120

I was at one of the conferences that the UK business held twice a year, in the spring and autumn. They were supposed to be a time for the senior team and a selection of established depot managers to have a business review and relax, and to a large extent they were. Over the years, however, the number of times someone did or said something silly, resulting in them never being seen again, had become a legend in itself. I used to thoroughly enjoy the events but was always secretly looking forward to just getting in my car to drive home again, still gainfully employed.

This particular conference was being held at the beginning of March 2018, in a large stately home in the Lake District, and the setting was breathtakingly beautiful. It was a pleasure to open the curtains in the morning and see the sun rising across the fields, and the mists tumbling down the valleys. It was even better when you could remember getting to bed the night before.

I looked at the agenda for the day. I was due to speak to the group, but as usual I was on right at the end of the morning session, when everyone was much more interested in what was for lunch and the activities planned for the afternoon than they were about the irritating little brother of a business that I presided over.

I went down to breakfast for a cup of tea and to find out if there had been any shenanigans after I had retired the night before. As I walked into the dining room, there were a couple of tables occupied with what looked to be deep, meaningful conversations taking place, so I found a table in a window, giving spectacular views across a lake, and sat alone.

Just as the waiter was taking my order, Bernard entered the room, walked to both of the deep, meaningful tables to say hello, then wandered over and sat with me.

'Good night, last night,' said Bernard. This told me in an instant that we probably still had a full team this morning.

'I thought so,' I replied.

When the waiter had left after taking both of our breakfast orders, Bernard was looking wistfully out of the window and said, 'I can see it now Peter, in the mist across the lake, 200 profitable depots in France. Can you see it?'

'I can Bernard, 200 horses galloping at full speed, and Napoleon at the front screaming *Ne passe pas!*'

This made Bernard laugh so loud that even the deep, meaningful tables stopped briefly to look at us. Some light chit-chat followed, before Bernard said, 'Seriously though Peter, I'm in a bit of an awkward position regarding France. You see, it's doing too well to close down, but not well enough to expand. I'm sure you can see the problem before me.'

I asked, 'What are your main concerns, Bernard?' to which he answered, 'Remember Peter, that I pay you to come up with the answers, but if I were you, I'd start by confirming that I'd got on top of the stock losses and debt collection, and I would then get the margin up... considerably.'

I replied, 'I understand Bernard, I'm pretty sure the first two are fixed now, and it's probably about time to address the margin now anyway.'

He said, 'Good, now if you'll excuse me, I need to make a quick call,' and left.

Shortly after that, my pot of tea arrived, along with Bernard's grilled kippers. Not knowing if or when he was returning, I stayed there for 15 long minutes, trying my hardest to avoid the pungent aroma of the smoky creatures on the plate next to me. I eventually had to give up though and went back to my room to quickly re-write my speech in line with my newly-discovered list of priorities.

121

I made a mental note to light-heartedly confront the eight people that sat doodling through my talk that hadn't been doodling through anyone else's, but apart from that, it went well. When I say well, I mean it was over quickly, and that was just about the only thing that anybody really wanted from me. I managed to squeeze my new short-term priorities in, and I saw Bernard almost smile at that point. A smile that said that his mission had been accomplished; the mission of getting the speech about France that he wanted – and all for the price of two cold kippers.

After everyone had demolished the hot buffet that had been prepared for them, and I had managed to find five of the eight doodling infidels, everyone was bundled onto a bus, which set off for a clay pigeon shooting range nearby.

Having been at many Eastney Interiors functions over the years, shooting clays was an activity that I was well used to. Bernard loved it and had all the kit, from the guns down to the shoes; he looked very much the country gent. For my part, I had become quite adept at it, usually finishing in the top half of any competition, but never taking it particularly seriously. My only gripe about it was that it could go on for a *painfully* long time on occasions. Luckily, this wasn't one of those times, and everyone was packed off in groups of six to shoot at five different stands.

In my team was Fiona. Her presence at the activity being an unusual occurrence, as her time at these conferences was usually fully taken up with preparing endless scenarios and spreadsheets that someone had just decided they needed as a matter of urgency.

Of the five stands, four were airborne, mimicking the flight paths of partridge and pheasant, both towards and away from the shooter. The last stand was rabbit, this being a ground level shoot, where the clay was propelled along the ground in front of the shooter, rolling on its edge like a plate.

Fiona struggled with the whole thing really. Partly due to being slight of frame so the recoil of the gun had a disproportionate effect, and partly because she hadn't shot as often as the rest of us. Much complaining was heard by the rest of our group as she only managed to hit three or four out of the ten clays on each round compared to everyone else's seven or eight. Her worst performance though, was the rabbit. She couldn't hit a single one. After ten missed shots, she declared, 'This is stupid, I wouldn't ever shoot a rabbit anyway, I don't like the taste.'

She then pondered for a few seconds and said, 'I like beef... I could probably hit a cow.' With this declaration of breath-taking logic, she handed the gun back to the instructor and got back on the bus to wait for everyone else to finish the stupid shooting without her.

The evening following the shooting was the last of that particular conference. I was on the home run and could almost smell the exhaust fumes as I started my car to begin the journey home.

As the evening progressed, a Mexican band started performing around the room in between the tables, wearing full traditional outfits, including very wide-rimmed sombreros. There were five players in the band and I was sure that I had seen them before somewhere. It was only later in the evening that someone mentioned to me that they had featured in some TV advertisements over the years. It being a Mexican themed evening, there were several full bottles of different flavoured tequilas on each of the tables and, during the meal, toasts were made and a different tequila was taken with each.

The meal ended and the band finished. A thoroughly enjoyable evening was had by all, and I left the bar to finish my packing and get some sleep. I could hear some people starting to sing songs back in the bar, and almost went back to join in, but decided against it. I arrived back in my room and laid back on my bed. I reflected that there was an energy, a truly tangible energy in that room and with that group of people, that I was struggling to emulate in France. I was creating the same environment, in so much as the building blocks were identical, it was just that the end result in France looked and felt quite different to the evening – and to be honest, the whole conference – that I had just experienced.

122

Back in McGuires with Claude and Sean the next evening, I was telling them about the conference, and specifically, Bernard's comments to me about scalability.

'Was he angry?' asked Sean.

I said, 'No, he was more concerned than angry.'

Claude said, 'The debt collection is certainly getting better, although we aren't up to UK levels yet. I'm not sure we ever will be, to be honest. The privacy laws in France are such that you can't get the background information on potential customers that you can in the UK to make a considered opinion on the level of credit we should extend. We are basically ploughing our own furrow on this one.'

'That's fine, Claude,' I said, 'you're doing a fantastic job.'

I turned to Sean and asked, 'What's the situation with the stock losses, if we wish to use that term?'

He said, 'I think we are on top of it. The two managers we got rid of had, by far, the biggest losses, and we think we've dealt with that. Regarding the others, I can't see any evidence of theft, but I can't absolutely rule it out of course. The recent stock audits are all in line with expectations. The one thing that bothers me though is that the two managers that we lost in December weren't two that I would necessarily associate with having each other as close friends, so there's still something that doesn't feel quite right, but as I said, the recent results are fine.'

I said, 'Can we not reclaim the cash from the customers that we can positively identify had unintentionally received free products?' to which Sean replied, 'No, I tried that, and as far as the law is concerned, it's our fault and therefore our problem.'

I said, 'OK, so if we put our rose-coloured spectacles on, we can see that the compliance issues are there or thereabouts. Next issue, and I suspect, the biggest, is the margin. How low are we Claude?'

Claude took a deep breath and said, 'That's a very good question

Pete, and it depends how you look at it. If you take the comparison to the UK based on...'

'Claude, could I please just have a straight answer?' I begged.

He adopted the look of a scorned puppy, and quietly said, 'We need to double it.'

I laughed and said, 'Do you know what I thought I heard you say just then, I thought you said that we had to *double our margin*!'

'Sticks, or carrots?' I asked as Sean and I were driving to the first depot the next morning.

'We usually use carrots,' was Sean's correct reply.

'Okay then, let's put some more money on the table to get the margins up,' I answered. 'Let's do it on a one-by-one basis though. We'll have a chat with the next manager we visit and set him some personal targets based on his own depot's performance and see where that gets us.'

'Absolutely,' was the reply from Louis at Englos depot when he was asked if he could get the margin up for 20 per cent more bonus. He agreed so quickly and easily that Sean and I decided to split up and try to cover all of the other depots in one day and have similar conversations with, hopefully, similar degrees of compliance.

Of the nine, seven replied in a similar manner to Louis, and two were a little more reticent, but agreed nevertheless that they would give it their best shot.

'Well, that was easier than I thought,' said Sean in McGuires at the end of a busy day's driving.

'Yes,' I agreed, 'but the margin didn't go up at all today, did it.'

Sean took a hearty slurp of beer and said, 'They couldn't realistically do much about today's margin. It'll take a few days to trickle down.'

I stared at him and said, 'Let's see what tomorrow brings then.'

At the end of the following day, Sean called me with the figures, but again, there was no move on the margin. He told a similar story to the day before about it taking a while to filter down, so I let it go again.

After a week of stagnant margin numbers, the conversation each evening between Sean and myself was getting a little more fractious. 'Are they even trying?' was my question at the end of the fourth day of zero improvement.

'Yes, or at least they are telling me they are. The story is the same everywhere, the margin will go up… soon.'

124

At a hastily arranged managers' meeting the following week in Lille, I was faced with nine managers that weren't smiling much. They still obviously had their various exchanges between themselves, and queued politely to get their essential caffeine fix, but when they were seated, they became quite passive.

I didn't want the meeting to be a negative one. What I really wanted to hear was that everything was under control and that the margin would be going up very soon. What I actually got though, was story after story of incidents where they had to drop their price to match, or beat, a competitor. When I looked into the individual deals that they had produced as evidence, it was clear that the products priced up by the competitor weren't anything like as good as our products, and when I pointed this out, all I would get was the standard Gallic shrug and comments about the customer not caring about our better specifications; all that mattered was price.

I tried to reason with them, by telling a story of a Rolls Royce salesman selling a car at the same price as a Honda Civic because, '...all that mattered was price.' They seemed to recognize this as a reasonable argument but didn't seem to be able to see any synergy between that story and the discussion we were currently having about their own margins.

At the end of the meeting, and as the managers were leaving the room, I turned to Sean and said, 'They are talking themselves into failure here. I could see that as soon as one of them had the balls to say that they had to keep dropping prices to close deals, they all jumped into his slipstream and followed suit.'

Sean agreed. 'Yes, maybe it's time for a few sticks, among the carrots.'

I decided to leave the heavy-handed tactics to Sean. Not due to an aversion on my part, but because if any of the tactics employed by Sean caused upset or complaints, I needed to be separate enough from the incident in question to be able to hear an appeal.

As it happened, that didn't ever become an issue. Sean tried the first stage of attempting to make them feel guilty about the low margins. That didn't work, so he moved onto emotional blackmail, where he compared the French depots to the depots in the UK. That was met with looks on their faces wondering why on earth that fact was relevant in the slightest.

Various other attempts were made by pitting one depot against another in a local margin battle with prizes along the way, and picking out the lowest margin manager every day for a few *home truths* about managing their business. All were met with the same dismal response.

Six weeks came and went. We tried everything that Sean and I knew how to, and each time we were met with the same result – nothing. I was questioning my own ability to run a team of people, and indeed a whole business. Sean was feeling the same, and his general mood was damaged even further when a few managers actually said to him that they didn't believe it was possible to get the prices up in the current climate.

At the end of May, I was in the Lille office with Sean, Claude and Henri. I asked Claude to give a brief summary of our abject failure to make any impact whatsoever on the depot margins. To be fair, he kept it down to about 30 minutes, which was almost a record for him.

I was making notes as Claude spoke, and when he finally finished, I thanked him for the clarity, but wanted to add a couple of other points. I said, 'I don't think we really know what the true market price is for our products if I'm honest. We are sitting here thinking we are cheap, but the underlying story in the field is one of consistently having to drop prices to beat a competitor, so until we can do some robust comparisons with the other sellers in the sector, we don't really know what the truth is. Sean, can you get some staff to get quotes for full kitchens from competitors that are comparable to ours, to see where we fit in, please?'

Sean said, 'Yep, no problem.'

I said, 'Hmm, if my experience of getting quotes is anything to go by, it will be nothing *but* a problem, but let's aim for ten different quotes on ten completely different kitchens please.'

I continued, 'The other issue we have to confront is that getting our selling prices up will require absolute buy-in from everyone in the depots. They have to *believe* that they can charge more for the kitchens than they currently do, and they have to *want* to do it; and that, gentlemen, is by far the bigger of the two obstacles that we currently face.'

I went out with Sean into four depots and listened to him asking the teams to go out and get kitchen quotes from other suppliers. Even this relatively simple request was met with long lists of questions about what exactly they were supposed to get a quote for. Whilst it was crystal clear in my mind, it obviously wasn't clear at all in the minds of the staff we were talking to. I pulled Sean to one side and said, 'We need to be careful here. If we aren't all completely on the same page about the objective, we will spend a lot of time getting data that is absolutely useless to us. We are going to have to give very specific instructions here, so that there is no room for misinterpretation.'

The two of us spent close to a whole day going through competitors' literature, establishing which suppliers and ranges were the closest to ours in terms of specification. We arrived at five different direct comparisons and decided to give each one to two depots in different areas, therefore giving the ten quotes. We specified which appliances, sinks and accessories they should ask for so that the quote we finally received would be as comparable to a kitchen of ours as was possible. With the detail finally established, it was a relatively simple message for Sean to then relay to the different depot managers. We asked for the quotes to be back with us within three weeks.

Believing our day to have been well spent, we were enjoying a curry in Lille that night. Claude joined us, as did Henri for a change. Henri wasn't a fan of Indian food, but made a valiant effort, even though he quietly ordered 'the mildest dish you have' from the waiter.

When the meal was over and the coffee had arrived, Henri said, 'Have you two given up on French food altogether then?'

I said, 'Not at all, we had a lovely meal in Belgium a few months ago, and I'm absolutely open to new suggestions, but food isn't my *raison d'être*, if you see what I mean. It's just a means of replenishing energy and shouldn't need too much thought.'

Claude said, 'So how many times a week do you two eat curry then?'

I gave it some thought, and said, 'I reckon two or three times a week here, and then another once at the weekend.'

Sean nodded and said, 'Same here. There's a good Indian restaurant near my home that I usually go to on a Friday night.'

Henri said, 'Your insides must look like an explosion in a paint factory. Have you seen how it stains the table linen?'

Sean and I laughed, and Sean said, 'I'd rather not think about that if it's all the same to you.'

Henri was about to push his point further, when Claude looked at him and said, 'Don't waste your breath Henri, they are both way beyond help.'

128

After the three weeks we had given the teams to get the kitchen quotes, Sean, Claude and myself collated the information that had been gathered. Of the ten quotes we had asked for, only one was completely ready. The other nine were still in various stages of execution. One of them was even still waiting for a salesperson to call her back from the initial call. When I asked why she hadn't chased it up herself, she insisted that she had tried to contact them again on several occasions.

The most common reason for the delays was the May staff exodus. I was finding the constant stop/start nature of corporate France incredibly difficult to deal with. It was almost impossible to get any sort of momentum going before the next wave of excuses to down tools kicked in. It was Claude who put this in perspective for me when he said, 'Pete, you expect France to dance to the rhythm of your business. It doesn't; it dances to the rhythm of family life.'

When I tactfully pointed out that a good family life needs the money that a business with good rhythm provides, I was met with the ubiquitous Gallic shrug and the somewhat depressing comment of, 'You need to choose your battles Pete, you've done well to get where you have so far with changing peoples' buying habits, but you will never change French values; not in a million years.'

129

In all, it took a full six weeks to get all the other suppliers' quotes gathered and verified. My observation that the process had taken so long that the price of the first couple of kitchens obtained were probably out of date now, was met with more Gallic shrugs all round. It would have to do though. If I tried to get the first ones re-done, I would be entering into 'Painting the Forth Bridge' territory.

Added to that was the fact that pricing on items like kitchens, cars, bathrooms etc. is quite fluid. If the salesperson is desperate for a sale on the particular day you walk into their showroom, you will likely get a better price than if the outlet had met all of their targets and were waiting eagerly for the next sales period and incentives. Eastney Interiors had built an entire business on that premise over the previous 15 years, so it would be hypercritical of me to complain about it. However, the idea of making strategic pricing decisions based on the information before me was a bit like building a house on shifting sands.

130

On the boardroom table in the office at Lille, I laid out the ten quotes that we had gathered from suppliers and the ten quotes that we had created for the closest 'like-for-like' that we could achieve.

Sean, Claude and myself were walking around the room. We had whiteboards spread around the room and I asked the two to just look at quotes and write anything that came to mind about any of them on a whiteboard. I explained that this wasn't the time for conversation, as that would come later. Conversation, at that specific time, might have persuaded someone to not write something down that they considered relevant, and I wanted as broad a spectrum of observations as possible.

After about 30 minutes, it became apparent that we had reached the end of our collective patience with this task. The visible signs were Sean looking around in cupboards for pens to steal and Claude tapping away furiously on his phone. I was no better; I had started doodling on the whiteboards myself.

We grabbed a coffee and sat down with the whiteboards in a row in front of us. I asked the guys what conclusions they could draw from our observations.

Sean started by saying, 'The take away for me is that the more you drill down into it, the less sense it makes.'

Claude nodded, and I had to agree with that sentiment myself. Claude added, 'I've tried to see if there is any logic or formula that we can apply to summarise it, and there just isn't.' More nodding.

In keeping with my general attitude to these things, I grabbed a flipchart and wrote the word 'Headlines' at the top of a clean page. I listed two things:

1 – We are cheaper than our competitors
2 – Our discounts are larger than our competitors

I said, 'The detail is very foggy, so we can't really build a proposal on the individual cases. The headlines though, are common throughout most, if not all of the quotes, and are things that we can do something about.'

'...like what?' asked Claude.

'Not sure yet,' I answered, '...but just think about the discounts for a start. Ours are in the 60 to 70 per cent range, that being because it's what the UK market likes to see. The French quotes all have discounts of 20 to 30 per cent. There *must* be something in that.'

Sean offered, 'Yes, but that's the builder's profit opportunity. If we reduce the discounts, we are reducing the amount that our customer can earn on any given project. That could screw our sales up completely.'

I said, 'Hmm', and carried on staring. There was something forming in my mind, but I couldn't articulate it at that point. I needed some time to think alone, so drew a close to the meeting and agreed to meet up for a curry that night. Sean and Claude left, and I just sat there, staring... and staring... and staring.

131

When I arrived at the Crest Hotel bar that evening, Sean and Claude were already there. Sean was just ordering a 'Vodka Martini, shaken not stirred' in his finest Connery accent, much to the amusement of the lady preparing the drinks. Claude was seated and had his laptop with him and open. By the look of the vessels by his side, he was halfway through his second glass of red and was tapping furiously on his keyboard as a result.

I grabbed a beer while Sean was still keeping the bar lady enthralled with his repertoire, although I was sure I saw her initial laughter turning into polite laughter with each soundbite that Sean offered. I did her a favour and called Sean across to where Claude and I were seated.

'Right then, Claude, what have you got for us?' I asked.

He said, '...give me two minutes, and I'll have it done.'

'Sounds exciting,' I replied.

Sean and I started discussing the day's sales, which were good, but the margin was still stubbornly low.

After more like 15 minutes than two, Claude said, 'Done it!'

I said, 'Done what, exactly?'

'I've made a spreadsheet of every one of the kitchen quotes we got from the competition and our own depots, broken them down group by group, you know, units, appliances, that sort of thing. Then I've calculated what extra margin we could get if we were to set our prices at just five per cent below the competitors, rather than the amount we currently are, which is up to 25 per cent in some cases, and arrived at a goal for our team to work toward. The sample size is relatively small, but it's all we've got to work with at the moment. If we can get these prices for our products, it will give us the extra margin we need to get Bernard off our backs and into expansion territory.'

Claude turned his laptop toward me, and I could see what appeared to be endless rows and columns of numbers. He started explaining the data and assumptions, but all I heard was white noise. I could see his mouth moving, but I couldn't hear anything he actually said. I interrupted him after a minute or two and said, 'Claude, I can see that this is the *what*, but the thing I want to hear is the *how*.'

Claude said, 'Well, that's kind of up to you two really.'

I couldn't help but think that we'd just wasted an hour of our lives. We'd already established that the depot teams were unable to get the prices up with the set-up we currently had, and me telling them how bad at their job they were and even providing endless spreadsheets proving that I was right, wasn't going to help.

I decided that it was time to put work behind us and go for our curry, wine, and some very important discussion about what makes the perfect holiday, to lighten the tone of the evening. Claude's preferred holiday was a traditional one; three weeks in the south of France with his family and plenty of rounds of golf. When Sean pushed him on why he wouldn't prefer somewhere like the USA or Spain, he just shrugged his shoulders and said, 'No, not for us thank you. The Côte d'Azur has everything we want from a holiday.' He clearly wasn't going to be budged on this matter, so we moved on.

Sean then contributed, 'My perfect holiday would have to be something like two weeks doing Route 66 with three or four mates on Harley Davidsons. It would be great to feel the wind in your face, with the beautiful weather and iconic backdrop.'

Claude asked, 'Can you ride a motorbike then?'

Sean looked down at his dinner and said, 'No, but I could learn!'

My own choice of the perfect holiday was simple. Two weeks staring at the TV from my sofa, with Garfield by my side and not a mobile phone in earshot...

I was back in the head office the next day. Sean and Claude were in Claude's office talking about depot governance and compliance, whereas I was still staring blankly at the jigsaw puzzle in the boardroom. There was too much information here. Anything I deduced or assumed could be disproven by some other piece of paper somewhere on the vast table in front of me. I needed to bring this down to bite-size chunks, or better still, just one chunk.

I walked over to Henri and asked him for the average selling price on our most popular individual kitchen unit, and what the average discount percentage we gave on that one unit was. Within ten minutes he gave me the information, and I made some space on the boardroom table for it. If nothing else, it gave me something different to stare blankly at.

My immediate observation was that the very high list price resulted in the average discount given being extremely high when compared to the French average of 25 per cent. I fiddled with a calculator for a couple of minutes and wrote some numbers down. I then stared at the piece of paper in front of me for a few minutes, before picking it up and walking into Claude's office and closing the door behind me.

It took me just two minutes to describe our plan to them, once I'd been able to articulate it to myself.

'You're a braver person than me,' said Fiona when I talked her through my plan. The change I wanted to make wasn't strategic, but was a significant tactical one, which meant that I was obliged to run it past the CEO before I did it. 'You know he's going to go ballistic, don't you?'

'Yes, it had occurred to me,' I replied nervously. 'When can you and Bernard be free for me to run through it with you both?'

She shuffled some papers and said, 'Let's do it this Thursday at 10am. If it's a problem with Bernard, I'll call you. Either way, I'll bring my tin hat.'

I half-jokingly replied, 'I don't suppose you have a spare, do you?'

I told Sean and Claude that we were going to London to see Bernard. I didn't plan on taking them in with me, but if Bernard needed some additional confidence about the proposition, I'd rather it was just outside the door than stuck in another country. It gave us a chance to have a decent dinner in London as well. They were both slightly nervous at the prospect, and I couldn't blame them. I had one shot at this, and my proposition was crossing a line that no-one in Eastney Interiors had ever dared cross.

134

We travelled over on the Eurostar on the afternoon of Wednesday 25th July 2018. It was a scorching hot day, and not particularly a day that you would want to be wearing the suits and ties that all three of us were.

We bunkered into our hotel just around the corner from the London office, got changed, and went straight to the pub. I've never been a fan of the '...better take it easy as I've got a busy day tomorrow' mantra. I'm more in the 'treat every day as if it were your last' camp. We spent the evening laughing about the day ahead of us tomorrow and imagining the possible outcomes. It had a 'Last Supper' feel to it, but I was determined that we would enjoy the evening. We all believed in the proposal that I was putting forward, and that it could deliver the increase in profitability that we needed to see.

135

6.30am and I was at the office in London. It was just two cleaners and me at that time of the day. I bagged a desk that was fully wired up so that I could connect and plug in my various devices. Sean and Claude rolled up at the ludicrously late hour of 7.45am, by which time the only available seats were at the big table in the kitchen area. I sat quietly laughing to myself, but changed my tune when I heard all of the raucous laughter coming from that general area, while I was sat in relative silence with all of my precious cables and peripherals.

I think it took about nine hours to get from 6.30 to 10.00 that morning. Time seemed to have adopted a whole new dimension in which to operate. Eventually though, Fiona's bright smile appeared out of one of the break-out rooms and, with a cheery 'Ready?', walked off at quite a pace in the direction of the boardroom, just expecting me to be immediately behind.

I gathered my papers as quickly as I could, and followed Fiona, almost breaking into a canter along the way. I could see Sean and Claude through the kitchen glass, and they both gave me a thumbs up as I sped by. I would have reciprocated, but trying to keep up with Fiona, holding my papers in one hand and a cup of tea in the other, somewhat precluded it.

When I reached the boardroom and finally got my breath back, I opened my file and prepared to tell Bernard of my plan. We started with some small talk about the business in general, which gave me the time I needed to get my opening gambit ready.

- 'So then Peter, I hear you have a plan to get the margins up in France.'
- *'Yes Bernard.'*
- 'Well go on then, I'm all ears.'
- *'I've got one sheet of paper to show you Bernard. There are reams of sheets behind this, but the story can be explained quite simply with this mathematical principle.'*

I gingerly pushed the one sheet of paper across the table and said, 'We haven't decided on the real numbers yet, but this shows where the opportunity lies.'

	Current	Proposed	Change
List price	50€	40€	-20%
Discount	40%	20%	
Nett price	30€	32€	+6%

Bernard picked it up and looked at it for a few seconds, and then put it down and sighed.

- 'So you're going to reduce the builder's earning opportunity. You think that's the way forward, do you?'
- *'I see it as amending it in line with the local market Bernard. As you know, builders didn't use to buy kitchens in France until we came along. They are used to seeing the lower discounts in the other outlets they use, and so the gamble is that they won't balk at a reduced discount from us. Other than that, it's just a normal price rise.'*
- 'Hmmm, smoke and mirrors...'

- *'Exactly Bernard, smoke and mirrors, I couldn't have put it better myself... except maybe smoke and miroirs.'*

I laughed nervously at my little joke and looked to Bernard for the smallest of smiles, but nothing was forthcoming. Not a titter.

- 'Am I right in assuming that the manager still has the final say on the price of each kitchen with each customer individually?'
- *'Absolutely Bernard, there is no change to the way our kitchens are priced; it is still a local decision by the manager on a deal-by-deal basis. We are just creating an environment where the manager can achieve a more realistic price for our products if he or she has the opportunity, because, as we know, our current gross margins are unsustainable, and the business will fold if we don't do something about it.'*
- 'How do you expect to capture the whole of the price rise?'
- *'Short term, attractive incentives for the managers to make hay while the sun shines. We will create new behaviours that, hopefully, will be maintained when the incentives end.'*
- 'There are a lot of variables in your plan Peter, and I'm very nervous about cutting customers' discounts. That's the builder's profit that you are eating into.'
- *'I know Bernard, but I believe we can make it stick.'*
- 'You do realise that if this fails, you will leave me with no option but to make some leadership changes, don't you?'
- *'Bernard, I wake up every day with that in my mind. In this business, we live by the sword and die by the sword. I would never expect it any other way.'*
- 'OK Peter, on that basis, I support your proposal.'

As Fiona and I left the room, she said, 'Well done Pete, he didn't explode.'

I replied, 'Yes, it was almost as if he already knew what I was going to say...'

With a backward glance and another cheery smile, Fiona walked into another meeting that was already in progress, sat down and started talking about a completely different subject.

'How did it go?' asked Sean and Claude, almost simultaneously as I entered the kitchen.

'It went well,' I replied. 'Well, in that he's supporting our initiative, but with the caveat being that it's the last chance saloon, for me at least. Anyway, that's the easy bit done, now we've just got to convince French builders that they want to pay more for our products, and French staff that it's possible.'

Claude said, 'I don't want to rain on your parade here guys, but we are now in serious holiday season, and getting something as major as this done is going to be extremely problematic.'

Sean laughed and said, 'Sometimes Claude, I think it's only your sunny disposition that keeps you going.'

137

That night, back in Lille, we went for a curry in our local. Claude spent a while on the phone placating his wife, Fleur, who was giving him a bit of a hard time about the number of evenings he was away from home lately. I had mentioned to him that it wasn't essential that he attend them, but he was always insistent that it was where he wanted to be. He reminded me that he had told me that he was looking for something like this when we first met.

We needed a timeline of all the jobs that we had to do. This included changing the prices on the system, printing new price lists and other literature, communicating the message of the 'price cut' to our customers, devising an incentive programme that encouraged our staff to capture the extra margin and, most importantly of all, selling the whole thing to our staff in such a way that they genuinely believed that they could do it.

I wanted the whole thing sorted by the end of the year. That meant that we had to get the price change in place for 1st October so that we had two months of the high incentive costs before we stopped them and found out if the plan had worked. December was going to be a tense time.

Over the curry, we established that Claude could get the systems and printing done by the middle of September. We decided that I would write to each of our customers explaining how the price review was going to affect them. This meant me signing several thousand letters, but I've always believed that one can recognise when a letter has been personally signed and that it is appreciated by the recipient.

As the food came and the wine did its work, we had a good night. We threw ideas around about what sort of incentives might do the trick, and about how best to communicate the message to the teams, most of which were ridiculous, but seemed like great ideas at the time. There were some nuggets of gold in their though, but I wanted to get as many wacky ideas on the table in one hit so that I could think hard about them when I got back to my room later. Sean said, 'We could try another car incentive...'

Some ideas were too preposterous to tolerate, so I had no alternative but to throw a half-eaten onion bhaji at him.

138

As the summer of 2018 did its annual job of bringing France to a complete halt, the three of us were concentrating solely on the plan for the autumn. Our own holidays had to happen of course, and for Sean and I that was a two-week break. For Claude, however, it meant a three-week break, the norm for most French people. He, like most of his countrymen, was travelling down to the south of France for his family *vacances* and copious amounts of golf. He did stay in touch though, secretly I suspect.

As it happened that year, Sean and I were able to take the same two weeks off, so that we could be back in the business together for the maximum amount of time. Sean was only going back to York to see family, so he was able to fit it in around my planned break. I was blessed to have two people around me who gave so much for our common cause.

Sean and I were in the head office one day during August. Claude was still off and it was barely noticeable that the business was functioning, with there being so few people around. We were still chewing the fat about the incentives and the means of communication. I was clear that I wanted a three-day, two-night trip somewhere in September to take the managers away and make them feel special, but I couldn't come up with an appropriate location. Sean, on the other hand had come up with a few ideas for incentives, but I felt that they were all too complicated.

We were staring at a map of Europe. I wanted the location to be special and memorable, but not overly expensive. I was looking at seaside resorts in Spain or maybe Turkey, when Sean said, 'What about London?'

I said, 'Not very exciting, is it?'

Sean said, 'Maybe not for us, but it will be for many of the team, and between you and I, we can create a great trip. And we can get there by train.'

I said, 'That's actually not a bad idea. Half a house point to you.'

A very disgruntled Sean said, 'Half a bloody house point! What am I supposed to do with that? When do I get the other half?'

I smiled and said, 'When you've got all the managers back to France afterwards with no casualties.'

He laughed and said, 'That's a heck of a lot to achieve for half a sodding house point!'

139

The very last person I wanted to discuss the incentives with was Claude. As an accountant, he was predisposed to always trying to get costs down, and for the most part, I agreed. There were times, however, when the short-term costs were irrelevant, and this was one of them. I am not one for management books or corporate mantras, but I do have a large, framed photograph of a very impressive seabird staring across a beautiful lake on the wall in my study at home. Along the bottom of it is a quote from an American consultant, Warren Bennis – '*Leaders keep their eyes on the horizon, not just the bottom line*', and it's a message that I remind myself of frequently.

As usual, and with my broad-brush approach to such matters, I drew a chart showing that if the managers captured half of the extra margin, they would get double bonus, and if they captured all of the available margin, they would get quadruple bonus. I made the mistake of texting Claude, asking how much it would cost, but allowing for the extra margin we would be making. It didn't take him long to get back to me with the message, 'My calculator doesn't have enough digits to calculate it.'

So... expensive then.

When I ran the idea past Sean, he liked it. He made a comment about it all being based on the managers though and asked if we shouldn't do something for the staff as well. I agreed and told Claude that we were going to extend the exact same scheme to all members of staff for the two-month period. His reply was, 'I hereby resign as Finance Director for two months, and wish to work in a depot.'

So... very expensive then.

The numbers were sufficiently high that I needed to tell Fiona about it. She was slightly bemused at how much I wanted to pay but agreed that the short-term pain was worth it if we could get the margin hike to stick. She made the point that it was still a big *if.*

When I added the cost of all the printing, and the trip to London, the numbers were eye-watering, even allowing for the extra margin we would be enjoying. It was not going to be a time for the faint hearted.

140

We started to form a plan for the trip to London. The first issue was the timing. The French holiday season is supposed to just crucify August, but in reality, the effects of it start in early July and end in mid-September, so finding a three-day window where everybody was going to be around was no mean feat in itself.

Eventually, with suitable dates found and a location decided upon, we could crack on with a plan. We needed to have some quality time to discuss the new initiative and the consequences of success or failure, but at the same time, I wanted the over-riding memories to be one of a good time had by all. A sort of *work hard, play hard* trip away.

Claude, on the other hand, was working around the clock getting our ducks in a row for the price change. He had to spend a lot of time on just arriving at the product prices themselves. He did this by taking the current average selling prices of each product as a start point, raising that by the percentage we needed, and then working backwards from there to arrive at the new list price, which, by virtue of the reduced discounts we would be applying, would be lower than it had previously been in every instance. It was a complicated process.

There was to be an additional benefit to our new reduced list prices, as Claude pointed out over a sandwich one day. He said, 'When we look at the discounts that the depots give, they seem to go up in five per cent increments.'

Sean said, 'Yes, that's the universal unit of discount, they will offer an extra five or ten per cent discount to close a deal on the day – never two percent or seven percent.'

Claude resumed, 'Yes, exactly, and with our new list prices being quite a bit lower than they were, the extra five per cent discount will now equate to fewer euros being deducted from the quote, and less damaging to the margin as a result.'

I said, 'So are you saying I'm a genius then Claude?' to which he smiled and said, 'I'd never say that Pete, never.'

The biggest problem for Claude though was getting all the new price lists and other promotional literature printed on time. Giving instructions like that to suppliers in France during August is almost pointless, as the mentality says that 'we'll deal with it when the holidays are over', so Claude had to physically go to the printer's office in Paris and explain how urgent it was that we got this particular job done on time, such that they diverted the miniscule resources they had available to the job in hand.

The systems implications were also sizeable. If we had been applying a universal reduction in price across the board, it would have been easy, but each product had to be adjusted individually, and with a depleted systems team in the office due to the holidays, it was very much a case of 'all hands to the deck'. I'm sure I saw the cleaner inputting prices at one point...

For all the difficulties, Claude said that we would be okay... just. It wasn't going to take much of a problem to throw his plans into a cocked hat though.

141

I had sat down a few times with a blank laptop screen in front of me, intending to write the letter of communication to our customers about the new pricing structure, and each time failed miserably. We had built up a good core of regular customers since we started, and it wouldn't take much to destroy all the hard work we'd done if they didn't like our plan

I sat down again in my room at the Crest one night before meeting Sean in the bar, determined to come up with *something.*

Dear (name),

Here at Eastney Intérieurs, we have been trading since 2016, and in that time have developed strong relationships with local builders like yourself with our model of local stock availability, credit terms, design service and confidential discounts. These discounts allow you to apply a handling charge on our products to your customer should you wish.

As you are aware, we are a part of a UK business that trades on exactly the same basis and, when we opened, we took the UK model and imported it in full, to see what worked.

Two years in, and we are still learning. We are still listening to our customers about how we can improve our offering to better help you be the person in your community that customers turn to first when they are considering a new kitchen.

One of the observations put to us by our customers has been that our discount structure is not necessarily aligned to the French market, with very deep discounts resulting in prohibitively high list prices. With this in mind, from 1st October 2018, we will reduce our list prices significantly, and align our discount structure to be more in line with discounts you see elsewhere in France.

We hope this helps you capture more of the kitchen market available to you, and that we can continue to develop our trading relationship further. If there are any other areas where you believe

we can help you secure more kitchen business, please do not hesitate to let me know.

(signature)

Peter Simpson
Président Directeur Générale

142

'That's not bad,' said Sean when I showed him in the Indian restaurant.

'Well, it'll do for a first draft,' I replied. 'Now then, what are you thinking we should do about the London trip? Any ideas?'

Sean replied, 'Yes, a few. I thought maybe the London Eye to start with, and then maybe a Duck Tour, which is part on road and part on the River Thames in an amphibious craft.'

'What about meals?' I asked.

'Well, we have two nights to fill, and I was thinking about an upmarket English meal, and maybe a Turkish one?'

That ticked all of my boxes for the trip, so I asked Sean to go ahead and arrange it. We would stay in a decent hotel near Waterloo Station so we could easily get to the attractions. It was also close to Covent Garden, where the atmosphere was frequently palpable.

143

We still had the small matter of current trading to worry about, and even though we hadn't officially told the depots what was happening, the business was small enough that everyone knew everyone else quite well and it was therefore almost impossible to keep our plan under wraps. I took the view that we would just say that we were 'reviewing our pricing structure in line with the local market' and leave it at that. I wanted the full details, and most definitely the incentives, to be a surprise when they got to London.

It was always difficult to gauge sales in August in France. Well, the general headline of *appalling* was a fair place to start, but which day of the week the public holiday on 15th August fell always made a difference to people's holiday plans, and therefore sales. Other things always seemed to have an impact as well; things like the weather, the current political situation, the school holiday dates… almost anything you could imagine would be cited as a reason why this *particular* August was poor. I had considered putting huge amounts of money on the table to defeat the annual exodus, but as Claude pointed out, it would have been pointless putting money on the table when there was no-one there to take it off again.

Nope, there was nothing that could be done. In the annual battle of Peter Simpson vs. France in August, there was only ever going to be one winner.

144

We eventually got through August, and slowly, more people were on the streets and in the depots, albeit in *la rentrée* mode, which in motoring terms is a speed just above idling. We saw sales pick up again, and it wasn't long before the holiday season was just a painful memory.

We had planned our London trip for the third week of September. This was largely due to staff availability, but it was convenient in that when the teams heard about the incentives, they had less time to delay sales from September into October.

Set over a Tuesday to Thursday, it gave the teams time to gather in Lille or Paris for the Eurostar that got into St. Pancras at about 2pm on the Tuesday. I then wanted to have the main meeting to inform the teams about the changes and the incentives almost immediately so that we had the rest of the time in London to get them excited about the earning opportunity and thinking about what sales and margins were possible within the two-month incentive period.

Wednesday was going to be basically an activity day, and then Thursday would be a debrief meeting before we got back on the Eurostar to France.

I had asked Claude to come along with us, but none of the other head office staff. I wanted this to be purely about the depot teams and not about support functions. Given some our previous experiences on trips away, the heads of department were not overly disappointed by this news.

145

With my (now considerable) experience of herding the managers around and allowing for escape groups of smokers, I had built plenty of time for lateness, problems and smoking breaks. This inevitably resulted in our being at Lille Eurostar station two full hours before we needed to be there. Sean had adopted the same policy in Paris and was equally early with the group that were departing from the capital. All this did was mean that people had too much time to kill, and wandered off into the station's facilities and beyond, such that when it was actually time to board, I was back to square one with trying to find everybody again. Back to the drawing board on that one.

With minutes to spare, I had rounded up the last of the smokers and arrived at the platform, and at the right place for our carriage. We had pre-booked our seats, and if everything had gone according to plan, we would be joining up with the Paris group, and our seats would be adjacent to theirs.

Our seats were adjacent to theirs, but two of them were already occupied. This was a common problem on the Eurostar when you weren't boarding at the train's initial departure point. People just decided to sit where they liked, on the basis that they will move if asked.

When we had been through the standard conversation of '...yes, it does matter to me that I sit there...' and '...I know it's only 90 minutes, but I still want the seat I booked...' we managed to remove the occupiers and assume our rightful positions.

There was already an energy among the troops. They knew that something was afoot and that it must be big, because they were being treated to a few days in London, but they didn't know what. It made a pleasant change to hear the occasional erupting of laughter among this group of people, whose more normal demeanour was one of reserved and philosophical contemplation. I whispered to Sean, 'I hope we can keep this energy up for the whole trip.'

He replied, 'Me too, but I hope more that I can get everyone safely back on the train back to France on Thursday with no casualties.'

I smiled and said, 'You really do want the other half of that house point, don't you?'

When we had arrived safely in London and got taxis to Waterloo, we checked in to our hotel and arranged to gather in the meeting room at 4pm. Claude, Sean and I went straight to the meeting room to make sure that everything was where we wanted it for the presentation. I was going to open, then hand over to Sean and Claude, and then I was going to close at the end.

I purposely wanted Claude to explain the maths. I had already told both Claude and Sean that no mathematical argument was going to get us the result we wanted, but that it needed to be made to give the whole presentation context.

When the team started arriving in the meeting room, they all, without fail, made a beeline for the coffee machine. Some things must just be instinctive, not actually a matter of conscious decision. There were obviously a couple still loitering outside with cigarettes, so Sean went out and hurried them up. Even those two still couldn't sit down until they had captured their caffeine fix though. The fact that they were the only two people in the room not seated did nothing to put them off from their pre-programmed course of action.

I welcomed the team and explained briefly what the agenda was. Sean then gave the details of the initiative, and how we hoped that the price adjustment would help us capture the extra margin. Claude then took over and showed how the maths worked and pin-pointed exactly where the opportunity lay, whilst still being the best priced kitchen supplier in France. He took about 20 minutes doing this, and I think it was only my noticeable and frequent watch-checking that kept him down to that.

I then took over again, thanked Claude, and said, 'The maths is clear. The opportunity is there. The question is – how can you make sure you capitalise on that opportunity? I will tell you – *Bonus!*'

I explained how they – and their staff – could earn double, or quadruple bonus for two months, and I could see the managers nudging each other and smiling. I made it very tangible for them by saying, 'Listen guys, if you can capture the full margin available, the extra bonus could easily buy you a new small car or a luxury holiday – it's completely up to you.'

I closed by saying, 'This isn't a mathematical exercise. This is a people exercise. It's about whether you can inspire your staff to get the proper market price for our products, in each of your depots. Can I have a show of hands if you think you can make that happen please?'

All nine managers immediately raised their hands, but more than that, they were smiling, and I could actually see belief in their eyes.

The chat at the bar before dinner on the Tuesday was all about extra bonuses, and not about a price rise. This was exactly what I was hoping for. This was just about people believing in themselves and, so far, it was looking good.

We set off on our 15-minute walk to the up-market restaurant Sean had booked in Covent Garden. It claimed to be the oldest restaurant in London, and whilst I had never eaten there, I had heard good stories about it.

We were met at the door by a reassuringly well-dressed doorman who checked our reservation before allowing us into the gastronomic emporium.

What followed was a feast to die for. Simple food but prepared and presented superbly. No raspberry coulis or coloured foam was to be seen – it would have just detracted from the quality of the meal. No hidden unidentifiable vegetables either, just normal accompaniments that balanced the main item perfectly.

I made a point of saying nothing to my French colleagues about – what I at least saw as – a far superior meal than anything I'd eaten in France, as I believed that the food should do the talking. The fact that the plates were all returned devoid of food and that the conversation throughout had been about the business and the bonus was, to me, exactly what a good meal should be about – the people, not the food.

We returned to the hotel. In taxis this time around as there were some wobbly legs as we left the restaurant. The French contingent were amazed at how easy it was to hail a taxi in London, given their experiences in their homeland.

Back at the bar, and I asked Sean to try to get the team up to bed by about midnight so that we didn't have too much of a job mustering the team in the morning. It was only a short walk to the London Eye, but I still wanted it to be an enjoyable day, and not one full of hangovers.

147

In my defence, no-one mentioned that Thomas from Massy was afraid of heights. If he or someone had, then he didn't need to go up in it. It was only when we were in the pod of the London Eye and had started our rotation, that it became apparent. Quiet mutterings of discontent turned into mild hysteria, which in turn developed into full-on panic and screaming. The only way to deal with him was to get him to lay on the bench that is in the middle of each pod and close his eyes. He was still sweating though, even though he couldn't see what was going on. I don't think the frequent comments from his colleagues about how high we were and how rickety the whole thing looked helped matters though.

The rotation took 30 minutes, but it seemed like three hours, with Thomas screaming like a banshee. He couldn't get off quick enough and ran to the water's edge to deposit his breakfast into the Thames. When he had calmed himself, I asked him why he hadn't mentioned his acrophobia, to which he replied, 'I didn't want to make a fuss.'

I said, 'It's OK, I don't think anyone noticed…'

Before the next activity, the Duck Tour, I made a point of asking if anyone was afraid of water. All eyes turned to look at a rather sheepish Thomas, but no-one expressed any concerns.

The tour was excellent, with a great guided tour as we drove around the streets of London, and then a ride along the Thames in the same craft. The vehicle entered the Thames rapidly from a slipway next to the MI6 building, which prompted a semi-scream from somewhere toward the back of the craft and gave Sean ample opportunity to add to the tour guide's commentary with his finest Sean Connery accent. I'm not sure that anything he said was factually correct, but at that particular moment, it didn't really matter.

It was while on the Thames that Claude asked me, 'Do you think they can capture the margin?'

I stared at the Embankment for a while, before answering, 'Short answer, yes. Longer answer, I think the chances of getting what we want while the bonuses are high are about 80 per cent, but I think that number decreases to 40 per cent when the bonuses end.'

Claude pondered that and said, 'Can we mitigate that risk at all?'

I laughed and said, 'I love the fact that your mind always goes to your safe-zone of mitigating risk, but this isn't really about cause and effect, it's about belief, it's about intangibles, it's about... human beings.'

Claude was about to offer another insight into the world of risk and reward when our craft bumped abruptly back up onto the slipway and resumed the tour along the streets of London, making him forget his train of thought.

149

With several managers of Turkish descent among us, I had high hopes that the dinner we would experience on the second evening would be a memorable affair. The restaurant appearance certainly didn't disappoint. It was a fairly small restaurant, but had the feel of a theatre about it, with drapes, balconies and even a stage area where they had performances while you ate. The menu was modern Mediterranean, with a lot of fish, and just a hint of a nod to the style of presentation that our French colleagues would appreciate.

With a couple of our managers speaking Turkish, we were treated like royalty and given a table running down the middle of the restaurant. Wine was placed on the table almost immediately and we began to soak up the surroundings and atmosphere. It was a beautiful place; the attention to detail with the décor was astounding, and many of us, myself included, walked around just photographing the little alcoves and swooping drapes that gave the restaurant a truly unique feel.

The meal was universally enjoyed, and as the last plates were cleared, a Turkish folk trio started playing from the stage at the far end of the restaurant. This prompted some of our group to stand up and start clapping along with the rhythm. This in turn led to some other guests following suit, until the whole place was on its feet, clapping and cheering along. Even the waiting staff were singing along while they worked; it was a truly wonderous experience.

I took this opportunity to quietly tell Sean that I would see him in the morning and reminded him about the remaining – as yet unclaimed – half house point. He looked at me, gave a thumbs up in the middle of his clapping, and carried on enjoying the moment.

As I left, Claude appeared behind me and said, 'I'll come with you, I don't think they'll be playing *Comme d'Habitude* anytime soon.'

150

The meeting was arranged for 9am, and the taxis for 10am to take us back to St. Pancras. There was nothing really to be said at the meeting, it was just a vehicle to get everyone up at a civilized hour.

There were some bleary eyes before me, but I did have a full set of managers which was a relief. However, it wasn't a full house; Claude was nowhere to be seen, and frequent calls to his mobile phone were just met with the answering service.

My heart was starting to sink when, at 9.15am, Claude walked in, apologised for his lateness and sat down. He looked fine, so I carried on with the meeting, summarising the objectives and rewards available. When I concluded, the group dispersed to gather their bags and I walked towards Claude. 'Everything OK?' I asked.

'Yes, sorry about that, I was on the phone. Bit of a problem back at base I'm afraid. We can't get any of the new price lists in time for 1st October.'

151

In a hastily arranged meeting with Sean and Claude in the back of a taxi, we were discussing the options available to us.

'How late will the price lists be?' I asked.

Claude replied, 'Two weeks, tops.'

Sean suggested we put the whole thing back by a month and let the incentives run for November and December. Whilst this was probably the sensible solution, I wanted to get the learning done in the current year, and not have the Christmas break between the end of the incentives and the real acid test of whether the gamble had worked or not in January. We had also just spent a couple of days whipping the guys into a state of excited frenzy, and I wanted to capitalise on that energy.

'Is there anything else we can do?' I asked, sounding slightly desperate.

Claude said, 'Well, the documents have been created, we know that. The delay is in the physical printing. What if we get soft copies of the documents from the design agency and email them to the depots? They can then print them off locally?'

Sean said, 'Not very professional, is it?'

Claude said, 'It'll do though for two weeks, won't it?'

Before Sean could reply, I said, 'Yes, it will do. As I've said before, this exercise is just about people, not prices... or price *lists* come to that. No, it's just about the people, and if they can do it at all, they'll be able to do it with home-made price lists for a couple of weeks. Well done, Claude, half a house point.'

Claude looked slightly bewildered by this unusual reward and was about to ask a question when Sean said, 'Claude, leave it, I'll explain later...'

152

The remainder of September was a strange time in the depots. There were still sales going through, although not at particularly high levels. There was an air of anticipation among the staff. It was like being in the eye of a storm, with a strange quietness among the troops. I was expecting there to be a lot of hustle and bustle with the preparing of sales for October, but it was quite the opposite. It was somehow quite unnerving.

On Monday 1st October 2018, I was nervous. More than that, I was petrified. We had done all that we thought we could to get the new prices to stick, and committed more money on incentives than we had ever done before. We had spent time with the managers and staff to make sure they really understood what we were asking of them and explained to our customers about the changes. That morning, however, it just came down to nine teams of people, and their ability to *sell*.

I was torn between going into the depots to see what was going on in real-time, or just leaving them to it and seeing the result at the end of the day. I opted for the latter and went to the office in Lille, where I spent most of my time pacing up and down like an expectant father. It being October, we were well into creating the budgets for the next year, so I sat down with Claude and went through some of the assumptions he was currently working to. I had hoped that this would take my mind off of things, but when Claude said, 'Pete, you've looked at your watch 14 times in the last half hour,' I realised that it hadn't and gave up with Claude's assumptions.

I called Sean to see what he was up to. He had taken refuge in the depot at Nanterre where there was a small office he could hide away in. He was being a lot braver than me though, in that he was keeping an eye on the sales and margin real-time via his laptop. I told him of my decision to make like an ostrich for the day, and all he said was, 'It's not looking too bad at the moment.'

Unlike me, he wasn't particularly nervous about today, it was the first day of December he was worried about. I told him that I was quite happy to worry about both equally.

I spent the rest of the day driving around competitors' outlets to see if there were any new products that we should investigate, or staff that seemed like they had energy and enthusiasm. It was certainly a better use of my time than putting everybody on edge at the head office.

Eventually and happily, the day finally ended, and I waited for Sean's daily telephone call to tell me the *scores on the doors*. The sales were high, unusually high, but Sean explained that the depots had indeed held sales back from September to get the better bonuses. Understandable, but frustrating. The margin, however, was up as well. Not as much as I'd hoped; we were in double bonus territory rather than quadruple bonus, but up none the less. When you factored in that the kitchen sales that had been held back from September had already had their price agreed under the old system, the picture looked quite rosy.

The following days told a similar story, but with fewer old sales polluting the margin numbers we were quickly into quadruple bonus territory, and above. This was fantastic news; it meant that the market was happy to stand the new prices and that our staff – for sky-high bonuses at least – were comfortable demanding the right price for the product. Sean and I were ecstatic, and Claude was too, well at least for most of the time. When he took time to calculate the bonus bill, he would look like he was about to cry.

At the end of October, our sales were well up on the previous year but, more importantly, we would be paying quadruple bonus in every depot. Bernard called to say well done, and I played it down with my concerns about December, to which he answered, 'Peter, in my experience of these types of things, you tend to know very quickly if it has worked or not.'

November followed suit, with sales being high and the margin still in the mega bonus vicinity. We now had a different issue. The depot teams were obviously going to try to squeeze as many sales into November as they could, to get the extra bonus. If that meant that they didn't sell a thing in December, that didn't really bother them as they would be up financially overall. Sean and I did what we could to talk the managers out of doing this, but to be honest, we might as well have been talking to a brick wall. The issue was a simple one. How would we know if we'd maintained the margin in

December if there were no sales going through to tell us?

So, it was through slightly gritted teeth that I was saying 'well done' to everyone on my depot visits during November. If you had offered me that predicament on the first day of October though, I would have bitten your hand off.

I had planned a managers' curry at Suri's for the last Thursday night of November. It was close enough to the end of the campaign to know approximately what the result was going to be, and I already knew that there was definitely some success to celebrate. It also gave me an opportunity to talk to the guys about December. I wasn't going to incentivise the margin anymore, but there was no reason why I couldn't incentivise the sales in the run-up to Christmas.

With the sales building a head of steam as we approached the end of November, and the margin holding strong, I was, bizarrely, wincing a bit myself as I saw the number of sales going through each day. I kept thinking that each sale might have previously been scheduled for the next month. I consoled myself with an old salesman's adage, which says that until a sale is in *your* till, a competitor can take it from under your nose.

154

I had given Suri the nod that we would be enjoying some Champagne on the night we were all there, so she made doubly sure that she had enough in stock for us. We saw the back of quite a few bottles between the 12 of us before a poppadom was even in sight. There were so many stories to celebrate and successes to toast that no night seemed like it could be long enough to fit them all in. Still though, in the back of my mind was the sales on the first day of December, so I made sure that Sean was toasting the successes of the past two months, and I was toasting the challenges and future successes ahead of us... starting on Monday.

The wine came, the food came, the digestifs came and the table descended into fits of laughter and song. Claude started off with his rendition of *Comme d'habitude* and Sean followed with a loud, and largely out of tune, version of *We are the Champions* which was joined in by all – at least for the chorus anyway.

155

For the second time in two months, I was nervously pacing around the office; this time on the first day of December. I had put some good incentives on the table at Suri's to keep the energy high, but the sales that the depots had put through on the last Friday and Saturday of November were staggering.

As I feared, the sales on the first day of December were very poor, but most alarmingly, so was the gross margin. I was beyond miserable when Sean phoned at the end of that day. I couldn't believe that all the effort and money I had committed had amounted to nothing. I was padding around my room at the Crest in Lille, planning my resignation letter in my head, when Claude phoned. 'Brilliant numbers today, Pete!'

I thought he must be being sarcastic, and just said, 'Yeah right.'

He said, 'No, Pete, they are great numbers. The sales are low, for sure, but the margins on every single product group are exactly as they were last month. It's only because fewer kitchens went through today that the overall margin is low. Pete, we did it... we *did* it!'

Whilst it was hugely reassuring to hear Claude's words at that precise time, and it did make my curry taste a little better that night, I still wasn't counting my chickens. The proof of the pudding, as they say, is in the eating, and until there were some kitchen sales going through, I couldn't actually bring myself to think positively.

It wasn't until the fourth trading day in December that we processed another full kitchen sale. There had been bits and pieces going through in the first three days, mainly due to customers changing parts for various reasons, and so the margins made on those small transactions wasn't necessarily representative of the underlying story. When the first full kitchen went through, Sean called me and said, 'It's looking good, full margin on a sale in Englos this morning.'

That was a relief, but even then, I still couldn't fully believe it –

it was only one sale after all.

There wasn't really a 'Eureka moment' for me during December. Every day, indeed every hour, I was half expecting the wheels to fall off and margins to sink again. I kept finding reasons in my head why it could still all collapse in a heartbeat. With every kitchen sale that went through though, I felt a little more positive. By the end of the second week in December, sales were back to normal for that time of year, and the margins were still at the levels we had targeted. Claude had been proven right. We had, collectively, managed to get the gross margin to a sensible level in one fell swoop.

156

As Christmas approached, Bernard asked me to present the details and findings of the margin exercise to the Executive Committee in London, as there may have been lessons for the UK business among them.

I did this in a fairly matter of fact way. I was over the moon with the results, but I didn't want to appear full of myself. If I've learned anything from being around Bernard for so long, it's that he detests hubris.

I'd probably been talking for almost ten minutes and was just getting to the part where I was going to summarise my findings when Bernard interrupted by saying, 'So what can we take away from this then Peter, in terms of what will be useful going forward?'

I replied, 'Well Bernard, I've thought long and hard about that, and I wish I could point to some earth-shattering conclusion that will unlock the rest of Europe for us. Unfortunately, or maybe fortunately I suppose, it comes down to the same things that have worked for us here. Firstly, it's about the people. In Sean and Claude, I've found two individuals that have given everything to make this work, even when the going got very tough. Also, without the managers and staff buying into the price rise, it would never have got off the ground. The other thing that made the difference was the short-term and very focussed incentives. The slight difference to the UK being that it's not the sort of thing I could put onto posters or announcements saying who has earned how much. It almost needed to be under the radar to be fully effective. *Our little secret*, I suppose you could call it. Maybe there's a lesson in that.'

On the last trading day of December 2018, Bernard called while I was driving back to Calais, I assumed, to wish me a Merry Christmas, which he did. After that though, he said, 'Peter, you've done well this year. You have also convinced me that the business is scalable and I will now support your plans for nationwide expansion. Present it at the next board meeting. Well done.'

I was lost for words for a few seconds, but finally managed a 'Thank you Bernard, I will.'

He then said, 'What are your plans for the first Monday we are back after Christmas?'

I told him that I was just going to Lille to sort out year-end stuff and to plan the sales campaign for January.

He said, 'Hmm, change your plans. Meet me in the Hotel Vermeer in Amsterdam at 4pm. – we've got a new international depot test to set up...'

Epilogue

Eastney Intérieurs continues to grow in France, and is now run by local operatives. Once the die has been cast and the local formula established, the job moves to one of compliance and procedure to ensure that the business doesn't digress from the founding principles. Whilst this may interest some, it doesn't particularly float my boat.

I moved onto new challenges within the company, and both Sean and Claude elected to come with me rather than stay within the French business.

Bernard retired in early 2021 and should really be enjoying plenty of very well-earned down time. Not one to rest on his laurels though, he now owns a chain of health spas across the north of England and Scotland.

Sean still sees Elise occasionally. I get the sense that it is very much on her terms, and when she is in-between partners. Sean seems to be quite happy with this arrangement, but as ever, doesn't talk about it very often which, to be honest, suits both of us.

Garfield and Boo-Boo went to the great kennels in the sky within about six months of each other, and both Claude and I were devastated. He has since bought a new puppy and called him Yogi (I can see a common theme here). I also bought a bouncy ball of fun and called him Sausage, much to the merriment of my friends, and the utter contempt of my wife.

When Sean, Claude and I need to go to France now, it is usually for a business event arranged by the local management, meaning that we eat in various French restaurants around Paris and Lille.

So that leads me to the thorny issue of food in France generally. Well, having eaten in many different restaurants now, I believe that the finest restaurant in France is Suri's Indian restaurant in Avenue des Ternes, Paris, and the best place to get quality French cuisine is...

Belgium.

PRINTED AND BOUND BY:
Copytech (UK) Limited trading as Printondemand-worldwide,
9 Culley Court, Bakewell Road, Orton Southgate.
Peterborough, PE2 6XD, United Kingdom.